THE APOS'
P⁄

MATERIALS FOR THE STUDY OF
THE APOSTOLIC GNOSIS

BY

THOMAS SIMCOX LEA, D.D.

VICAR OF ST. AUSTELL

AND

FREDERICK BLIGH BOND, F.R.I.B.A

AUTHOR OF "THE GATE OF REMEMBRANCE"

PART II.

SECTION I.

INTRODUCTION
THE TEMPTATION
THE MIRACLES
NOTES ON THE CLEMENTINE HOMILY

SECTION II.

NOTES ON THE CLEMENTINE HOMILY
ST. PETER'S CONFESSION
THE TRANSFIGURATION
THE ANNUNCIATION
THE 37 MULTIPLES

RESEARCH INTO LOST KNOWLEDGE
ORGANISATION

c/o R.I.L.K.O. Books,
B & J Hargreaves,
10 Kedleston Drive,
Orpington,
Kent. BR5 2DR

Distributed by
THORSONS PUBLISHING GROUP LIMITED
Wellingborough, Northamptonshire

First published 1922
This Edition published 1985

Foreword © WARREN KENTON 1985

British Library Cataloguing in Publication Data

Lea, Thomas Simcox
    [Materials for the study of the Apostolic gnosis].
    The Apostolic gnosis.
    Pt. 2
    1. Bible. N.T.—Criticism, interpretation
    2. Gematria
    I. [Materials for the study of the Apostolic gnosis]
    II. Title   III. Bond, Frederick Bligh
                    225.6'8   BS2990
    ISBN 0-902103-10-5

Printed and bound in Great Britain

CONTENTS

FOREWORD

It is said that the Bible has many levels of comprehension. This is what makes the scriptures quite different from ordinary literature. The first level is that of the plain meaning where every incident is seen as actually having happened and is to be thought of as a history. The second level is allegorical in that the events described are symbolic and the people involved are archetypes. This is manifest in many Biblical names like Joshua which means "The Deliverer", Jesus is the Greek version. The third level is the metaphysical. Here number and structure, form and dynamic are perceived to run through the text to reveal a beautiful system of correspondences and unfoldment that underlies events and people who are acting out a profound drama which the reader might ponder and perhaps glimpse or comprehend the mysteries present.

Gematria or the study of numbers and their relationship to letters and words originated in Babylonia. It was adopted by the Greeks and later still by the Jews of the second temple period. It was a method by which connections between theme, idea, place and people could be made to deepen the understanding of what was written. If used in conjunction with the literal and allegorical methods many insights can be found in the familiar stories and characters portrayed in the scriptures. This can lead on to the fourth level of awakening when the scriptures become *revelatory and alive* as one sees them present in the world of today. The fifth level is to recognise that they are also within oneself and relate to ones own development as a soul. The sixth level is to perceive the cosmic dimension of the text and how we are all involved in a spiritual reality in which history, allegory and metaphysics are fused into the flow of creation and manifestation of Divine Will. The last level is the direct contact with the Holy One. Here everything is seen as a reflection of God so that word, symbol and number disappear in the realization of I AM THAT I AM. This book with its detailed analysis offers that possibility to the perceptive reader.

Warren Kenton
WARREN KENTON

PREFACE

THE contents of Part II. of this work do not exactly correspond with those adumbrated at the commencement of Part I. The words of Power accompanying the Miracles are dealt with, and some parts of the mathematical symbolism will be found under the head of the Miracles of Unseen Escape and in the notes on the 17th Clementine Homily. But much is still held over being as yet imperfectly verified or worked out. Ὀθόνη μεγάλη has the number 294, which is that of ἐκκλησία, of ἡ καλὴ παραθήκη, of ὁμολογία and of ἡ σκήνη. It is clearly the Church. And κατάβαινον σκεῦός τι, 1710, is the number of πνεῦμα ἅγιον Κυρίου. The number of Θῦσον is that of Κηφᾶς, 729, and Θῦσον καὶ φάγε· "Slay and eat," 1269, is δεῖπνον Κυρίου, the Lord's Supper. But we are certain that there is far more than this in the Vision, and prefer to postpone publication.

As regards the Epistle to the Hebrews the work is far advanced but is enough for a volume by itself. If we propound as its conjectural title Ἡ πρὸς Ἐβραίους ἐπιστόλη Ἀπολλώ we get the significant number 2960 which we publish in the series of multiples of 37 and which can stand here for Θεότης Ἰησοῦ Χριστοῦ. And when we come to the word τετραχηλισμένα we suggest that this has nothing to do with τράχηλος, a neck, but is the perfect passive participle of τετραχηλίζειν, with the reduplication eliminated by the known principle of "haplology." It will then mean not merely πεφανερωμένα as Hesychius gives it, but "cleft in four planes." Likewise concerning Melchisedec there are many things hard to utter, but both "the grace" ἡ χάρις, and "the help in time of need" ἡ εὔκαιρος βοήθεια, have his number of 919.

Miscellaneous examples are very numerous in our collection, and it is difficult to sort them into order for exhibition. "A babe wrapped in swaddling clothes"

Βρέφος ἐσπαργανωμένον is Κύριος Ἰησοῦς Ἐμμανουήλ and "lying in a manger," κειμένον ἐν φάτνῃ, is Υἱὸς Θεοῦ, Son of God. There is more there. Instead of the Magnificat, which has too many cases of the doubtful final ν, we publish the Annunciation message of the Angel, a glorious miracle of verbal inspiration. Many examples must await the full treatment of the "Testimonies," or quotations from the Septuagint which were regarded as prophecies that the Messiah should suffer and as proving that Jesus is Messiah.

One more matter of a much wider scope must be mentioned. It is now more than ever borne in on the authors that their work is an appeal to Greek as against the dominant Latin tendency of the last fifteen centuries at least. The Latin genius has made for clear-cut teaching on deductive syllogistic lines, enforced by discipline in legal form. The intellectual feature of the present time is inductive science, reasoning upwards from facts rather than downwards from dogmas. It is the glory of the Latin Church that it converted the Western barbarians. It is the shame of the Greek Church that it did not carry the Gospel to Arabia and Persia at least, if not farther. Hence the scourge of Mahomet. But we, the authors, believe that it is possible to teach the Christian faith inductively from facts; that the Lord and His Apostles did this; and that the Church of to-day can follow Their steps, and teach on Their lines. It should be possible. Each of us has had some training in the scientific methods of the day, and to apply those methods to the study of Holy Scripture is neither unreasonable nor unpromising.

A list of corrigenda in Part I. has been inserted in copies of that book which remain unsold. It is also given here. The utmost care is taken in this Part to avoid miscounts and errors, but some mistakes may still be found and for these we crave indulgence.

APOSTOLIC GNOSIS.

PART I.

———

LIST OF ERRATA,

also of certain miscounts discovered, for which alternatives are given.

p. 20. For *gift of spiritual expression* read *gift of spiritual conception and expression.*

p. 69 and following, in the lists of 2368, equivalents of Ἰησοῦς Χριστός, under the numbers given read :—

No. 43.   For Ζωὴ ἐκ πατρός read ὁ λόγος ἐν κόσμῳ.

No. 143. For δεσία read δέξια.

No. 237. For *Son of the Kingdom* read *Sun of the Kingdom.*

No. 318. Add 318a. Μετακυβικὸν πρόσωπον,—Meta-cubic Aspect or Face.

No. 379. For Ἡ ἀόρατος ἐκκλησία · οἰκοδομία Κυρίου read ἀόρατος ἐκκλησία · οἶκος θεότητος.

No. 380. For this and the two following examples, *i.e.* 381 and 382, read :—

   380.   ἀόρατος ἐκκλησία · οἱ σωζόμενοι.
          Church Unseen : the Saved.

   381.   ἀόρατος ἐκκλησία · ἡ ζωὴ ἐκ Θεοῦ.
          Church Unseen : the Life from God.

   382.   ἀόρατος ἐκκλησία · ἡ ἄνω γένεσις.
          Church Unseen : the Birth from above.

No. 415. For σύγκλεισμα καταπετάσματος read
ʽΗ κατοίκησις τοῦ Πατρός.
The Abode of the Father.

No. 466. Add 466 a. Φωνὴ παρακλήτου. Voice of
the Comforter.

No. 475. Substitute :—
Ἀλήθως θεὸς · ἐνοίκιον Πατρός.
Very God : Habitation of the Father.

The following also may be added to the Eucharistic
series :—
ʽΟ ἄρτος οὐράνιος · ὁ Μεσσίας.
The Heavenly Bread : the Messiah.

ʽΟ ἄρτος σταυρότυπος.
The Bread (wafer) marked with the Cross.

Δεῖπνον τῆς σαρκὸς Κυρίου.
Supper of the Flesh of the Lord.

p. 108. Omit footnote.

p. 118. Add under 2220.
ʽΗ ἐπίγειος οἰκία τοῦ σκήνους. (II Cor., v. 5.)

NUMERAL ALPHABET.

WE know of course that the Greek alphabet was used to express numerals, and that the numeral values of the letters were and are as follows :—

A α	.	1	N ν	.	50
B β	.	2	Ξ ξ	.	60
Γ γ	.	3	O o	.	70
Δ δ	.	4	Π π	.	80
E ε	.	5	P ρ	.	100
Z ζ	.	7	Σ σ	.	200
H η	.	8	T τ	.	300
Θ θ	.	9	Υ υ	.	400
I ι	.	10	Φ φ	.	500
K κ	.	20	X χ	.	600
Λ λ	.	30	Ψ ψ	.	700
M μ	.	40	Ω ω	.	800

INTRODUCTION TO PART II.

IN publishing this second part of the materials for the Study of the Apostolic Gnosis the cumulative effect of the large number of instances emboldens us to state hypotheses of a more definite character. We have arrived at this point largely through a survey of the gematria found in the "Words of Power" used in the Miracles; the "Testimonies" from the Prophets, etc.; and our research included a detailed examination of the Epistle to the Hebrews. Of this latter book we have in preparation a detailed study, but find it is not possible to include this in the present volume. We must therefore content ourselves with the offer of a few remarks which would seem pertinent here. The Epistle to the Hebrews is conjecturally attributable to Apollos, and from the notices in the Acts it seems certain that Apollos had a very effective method of assisting the spread of the Gospel. He watered where St. Paul had planted, and helped them much who had believed through the grace, for he mightily convinced the Jews and that publicly, showing from the Scriptures that Jesus was the Christ. He was an eloquent or learned man, "mighty in the Scriptures," a Jew from Alexandria, who knew about the Baptism of John before he understood from Aquila and Priscilla the fuller doctrine taught by St. Paul, and quite possibly heard from St. Peter also, when Aquila and Priscilla had been in Italy, before the edict of Claudius had caused their emigration. And it seems possible to conjecture how he argued. Unless it be in the Epistle to the Hebrews, there is none of his teaching extant. But there are passages of St. Paul's Epistles which may be on the same model. One or more instances from Romans xv. (being the Epistle for the Second Sunday in Advent) may be used as illustrations, for St. Paul is there on the same quest. There would be no objection to regarding the passages quoted from the Septuagint as Messianic; nor, except among the very extreme Hebraists, who would be rare among the Dispersion, was there lack of a disposition to regard the Septuagint as an inspired translation. But the particular point of the Apostles' insistence was that Jesus of Nazareth was the Christ or Messiah. How could that be proved from the Septuagint? The mere recital of the passages quoted hardly gives the clue. But if he could show the gematria thus :—

"Rejoice, ye Gentiles, with his people"

Εὐφράνθητε ἔθνη, μετὰ τοῦ λαοῦ αὐτοῦ.   4238

= The light of Jesus Christ!

Τὸ φῶς Ἰησοῦ Χριστοῦ.   4238

or

"The Advent of the Lord Jesus Christ"

Ἡ παρουσία Κυρίου Ἰησοῦ Χριστοῦ

he would certainly be giving point to his argument.

Or again :

"Praise the Lord, all ye Gentiles, and laud him all ye people."

Αἰνεῖτε πάντα τὰ ἔθνη τὸν Κύριον

καὶ ἐπαινεσάτωσαν αὐτὸν πάντες οἱ λαοί.   5638

= Jesus Christ the Light of the Lord.

Ἰησοῦς Χριστὸς φῶς τοῦ Κυρίου.   5638

or

The Saviour, the Revelation of the Light.

ὁ Σωτήρ.   ἡ ἀποκάλυψις τοῦ φωτός.

Or again :

Ἔσται ἡ ῥίζα τοῦ Ιεσσαί καὶ ὁ ἀνιστάμενος

ἄρχειν ἐθνῶν,   4546

= Mystery of the Lord Jesus Christ.

Μυστήριον Κυρίου Ἰησοῦ Χριστοῦ.   4546

and when the remainder of the quotation is added

ἐπ᾽ αὐτῷ ἔθνη ἐλπιοῦσιν.   2513+4546=7059

with the interpretation

Ἀνατολή ἐξ ὕψους· σωτηρία τῶν ἐθνῶν πάντων

h℈ would be able to show the total as representing Jesus the Nazarene in the flesh, the Son of the Substance of the Lord God.

Ἰησοῦς ὁ Ναζωραῖος · Σαρξ καὶ Ἁιμα
Ὁ υἱὸς ἐκ τῆς οὐσίας τοῦ Θεοῦ Κυρίου

or

Ἰησοῦς Χριστὸς ὁ Ναζωραῖος ·
ὁ Μεσσιας ἐκ πατρὸς · Ὁ υἱὸς ὁμοούσιος.

The other quotations will yield similarly significant results, but these will suffice for the moment. The effect must needs have been disquieting. Such arguments must be met, if only by some variation of the *argumentum baculinum.* They could barely be tolerated in a Hellenist Synagogue. Jerusalem would be frantic. The stern descendants of the Exiles of Babylon were indisposed to treat Hellenists or Refugees of Egypt very cordially. They would see the gap in the argument and would refuse to have it bridged by counting Greek letters. And many Christians of our day would be of much the same opinion. But the existence of the possibility could not then and cannot now be denied. There are such countless instances of it. Can it be that the Lord stored up in secret in the words of a translation the prophecy that Jesus of Nazareth would come and be revealed as the Son, the coequal and coeternal God? And yet it would seem a literary impossibility to restate, as it were in duplicate, a great system of theology and mathematical philosophy so as to make possible a constant correspondence between letter and number. Yet here is an example of such a system set forth.

It is not claimed in the above instance that the interpretations given are those that St. Paul put on the texts. Indeed it is even more than probable that he had others. But there is a case in the Pistis Sophia where probability verges on certainty that the Christians did have such a system, and that what must have been their interpretation has been recovered.

Most readers of this book will be aware that the
85th Psalm (Ps. 84 in LXX) is proper to Christmas Day.
It contains the words

"Mercy and truth are met together,
    Righteousness and Peace have kissed each other.
    Truth shall flourish out of the earth,
    And Righteousness hath looked down from heaven."

And this passage is interpreted by the disciples in the
Pistis Sophia at considerable length as relating to the
Humanity and Divinity of the Lord. The basis is
a story, which must be allowed to be wholly apocryphal,
of an alleged incident in our Lord's Infancy, where
a spirit in all respects the exact double of the Lord
meets Him, and the two embrace and become one.

The references are Ps. 85, 10, 11; Pistis Sophia pp. 121, *sqq.*

"Mercy and Truth are met together."

Ἔλεος	310	Χριστὸς	1480
καὶ	31	Μαριάμ	192
ἀλήθεια	64		——
συνήντησαν	1267		1672
	——1672		——
		Οἴκημα	149
		Κυρίου	1000
		ἡ	8
		Παρθένος	515
			——
			1672

The meeting of herself with Elizabeth is also referred
to by the Virgin as interpreting Mercy and Truth in
another fashion, and it is noteworthy that

Ἐλισάβετ   553
Ἰωάννης   1119
            ——
      = 1672

"Righteousness and peace have kissed each other."

δικαιοσύνη	773	Κύριος	800
καὶ	31	ἄνθρωπος	1310
εἰρήνη	181		
κατεφίλησαν	1125		———
	———2110		2110

and the whole passage		Μεσσίας	656
	= 1672	Κυρίου	1000
	+2110	Χριστὸς	1480
	———	ἔνσαρκος	646
	= 3782		———
with the interpretation.			3782

Note on 2110. This is also the gematria of "The breaking of the bread," Ἡ κλάσις τοῦ ἄρτου, 2110, where heaven and earth, God and Man, may also meet, and

ἡ σὰρξ Κυρίου (the flesh of the Lord)	1369
ὁ ἄρτος (the bread)	741
	———
	2110

"Truth flourished out of the Earth."

Ἀλήθεια	64	Τὸ	370
ἐκ	25	σημεῖον	383
τῆς	508	Γυνή	461
γῆς	211		———
ἀνέτειλε	406		1214
	———1214		

= ἀνέτειλε	406	Ἡ Εὖα	414
Ἀλήθεια	64	Κύριος	800
θεοτόκος	744		———1214
	———	ἡ μήτηρ	464
	1214	ὁ υἱὸς	750
			———
			1214

"And righteousness looked down from heaven."

Καὶ	31	Μεσσίας	656
δικαιοσύνη	773	τοῦ	770
ἐκ	25	Κυρίου	1000
τοῦ	770	Σωτήρ	1408
οὐρανοῦ	1091		——3834
διέκυψε	1144		
	——3834		
	5048		5048

Ἰησοῦς	888	Μυστήριον	1178
ἡ	8	τὸ $\}$ (or φωτός)	
ἀποκάλυψις	1512	φῶς $\}$	1870
τοῦ	770	ἐξουσία	746 ⎱
φωτός	1870	τοῦ	770 ⎬ 2000
		θεοῦ	484 ⎰
	5048		5048*

The Pistis Sophia makes it quite clear that Ἀλήθεια
refers to the Virgin and the Lord's Human Body, the
interpretation being put into the Virgin's mouth. We
can have here nothing less than a fossilised trace of
the very early connection of the 85th Psalm with the
Incarnation. And to our aid comes no less a person
than the great St. Athanasius who, in his commentary
on this psalm, says "Clearly he proclaims the truth that
arose on the world through Theotokos Ever-Virgin."

And it has been already shown that the more
celebrated prophecy of Isaiah can be interpreted to bear
on the same subject by the same system. (Part I, p. 109.)

---

* *Note on* 5048. There is also a Gnostic interpretation of this number
assigned to St. John in the Pistis Sophia, Μίκρος ΙΑΩ Σαβαὼθ ἀγαθός, 2548,
with 2500, φῶς Κυρίου, giving the number. 2548 is also Τὸ μυστήριον κυρίου.
Power from this entity is stated to have been placed in the Baptist. But
there is a similar, though higher, power in the Lord's Body (Pist. Soph.,
pp. 13, 14). This one is seemingly Μέγας ΙΑΩ Σαβαὼθ ἀγαθός with the
number 2357 (2 × 1178·5) which is, by gematria, λόγος θεοῦ κατὰ μυστήριον.

Now the first form that opposition to the theory took in our own minds was that these were merely accidental coincidences. This was quickly disposed of when we found what an enormous number of such cases there were. So next it became a question whether any number would not give us similar results, showing, that is to say, a gematria of special nature, with strictly appropriate parallels under each number. But even if that were so the marvel would not cease to be marvellous, for what could this wondrous scheme of religious teaching be to which every combination of letters in the language in which it was preached bore witness? Not that it is so by any means. There are some numbers that seem entirely without significance, while there are others again which have a very large gematria. But it may very well be asked whether any other religious or philosophic system can show such a very remarkable peculiarity. It is proverbially difficult to prove a negative, but no other has appeared to our knowledge except the Pythagorean and Platonic mathematics which are seemingly incorporated with the religious doctrine or idea of Creation.

Nevertheless there is in Iamblichus vii. 4, 5, a statement that the Egyptians held that the names of the Gods contained the attributes of the Gods, and that translation of these names destroyed their meaning. So the idea was in existence. But to St. Irenæus it seemed absurd to suppose that a name from another language should be transferred to a Greek numeral system with any idea of retaining its intended significance. Yet it was done in both the names of Ἰησοῦς and Ἰωάννης. It is difficult, to us at least, to avoid some theory of verbal inspiration, or something of the nature of "tongues" as a spiritual gift.* St. Paul is careful to explain to the Corinthian Church how secondary and transient and partially distributed were these secondary charismata. The word he uses, καταρ-γηθήσεται, means "shall become idle" or useless for work, and it cannot be supposed that a knowledge of Greek numerals could have been the sole key to the interpretation of the Divine Mysteries. Therefore there must have been, behind the Greek, some more universal means of acquiring, through intellectual channels, the knowledge necessary to salvation; some method of ex-position that could lead on to higher knowledge, and could be truly and adequately stated in every language of every age. Essentially we hold that the system of teaching which makes use of mathematical and geo-metrical symbol for the inculcation of the higher truths of religion is precisely such a universal method; and that when once implanted, it may dispense with the aid of its foster-mother, the "tongue" that guarded it in its inception. But a survey and careful analysis of truths imbedded in the "tongue" may still be a sign to the unbeliever, and therefore may well be known to the believers, even after it has ceased to be of use to the believers themselves when their faith is advanced to knowledge. Nevertheless, so long as it can be shown by the gematria, even in a single instance, that through the premature loss of this method, an incorrect or mis-taken sense has been, in the latter days, imported into the meaning of any word (such as γνῶσις, μυστήριον,

---

* *Note.* The better to explain to the reader the nature of our contention, we will state a possible line of argument as to the "interpretation of tongues." This, in the Church, was the work of men specially qualified and skilful. They would discern parallels through their knowledge of affinities of meaning, and we find numerous instances of such affinity of meaning in the actual gematria of Hebrew and Greek words and names to be educed by comparison.

The tongue may vary, but behind the tongue is the universal symbolism of Number whose terms are unchangeable and constant. Hence the inter-pretation remains true so long as the language lasts uncorrupted, and so long as the sacred records are not tampered with by the copyists this power of interpretation remains in the writings.

μετάνοια, etc.), we claim that this method of exegesis cannot safely be dispensed with, as it has not fulfilled its possibilities nor exhausted its uses.

It has long been a problem how to bring religious faith into such touch with intellectual knowledge that faith becomes a probable extension of what is already certainly known. We know in part and ought to be able to prophesy in part, aiming after that which is perfect and which is to come.

But the problem undoubtedly is beset with difficulties. A good series of examples of these will be found in St. Paul's sermon at Antioch in Pisidia, Acts xiii, 16.

The Scriptures he quotes give, as they stand, fine gematria, but they are not all exact quotations from the texts we have now. In the first, which is "I have found David, the son of Jesse, a man after mine own heart who shall perform all my will." (Verse 22.)

Εὗρον Δαβίδ τὸν τοῦ Ἰεσσαί, ἄνδρα κατὰ τὴν καρδίαν μου, ὃς ποιήσει πάντα τὰ θελήματά μου.   5784.

This gives

Ἡ ἐπαγγελία. φῶς τοῦ Κυρίου Ἰησοῦ Χριστοῦ.

5784.

And

Ἡ διαθήκη Κυρίου, τὸ μυστήριον κεκρυμμένον Ἰησοῦ Χριστοῦ.   5784.

But one looks in vain for the exact passage.

The second is the great text "Thou art my Son, this day have I begotten thee." This appears again in the Epistle to the Hebrews where a strong argument is based on it. It will suffice to show here that it contains the name of Jesus.

Υἱός μου εἶ σύ, ἐγὼ σήμερον γεγέννηκά σε.
680 + 510 + 15 + 600 + 808 + 473 + 145 + 205 = 3436.
Ἰησοῦς τὸ μυστήριον Κυρίου.
888 + 370 + 1178 + 1000   = 3436.

This is quite correctly quoted from the Septuagint.

In the same way, "I will give you the sure mercies of David"

Δώσω ὑμῖν τὰ ὅσια Δαβὶδ τὰ πιστά.   3799
will give

Ἰησοῦς ὁ ζῶν, φῶς Θεοῦ.   3799.

This is very interesting, as Ἰησοῦς ὁ ζῶν is the title of the Lord in the Bruce Codex. But here in the LXX. it is διαθήσομαι ὑμῖν διαθήκην αἰώνιον and not δώσω.

The next, "Thou wilt not suffer thy Holy One to see corruption" can pass, for the only alteration is οὐ for οὐδέ.

Οὐ δώσεις τὸν ὅσιόν σου ἰδεῖν διαφθοράν.   4003
will give

Μυστήριον Κυρίου, ἡ ἀνάστασις καὶ ἡ ζωή.   4003
and

Ἰησοῦς υἱὸς τοῦ Θεοῦ ἄφθαρτος.   4003
= Jesus, Son of God Incorruptible.

The next, which differs considerably from Habakkuk I, 5, which is the nearest to it, and where the vague description "said in the prophets" is used to introduce it, is very long, but divides into clauses thus (Acts xiii, 41).

"Behold ye despisers, and wonder and perish."

Ἴδετε οἱ καταφρονηταὶ καὶ θαυμάσατε καὶ ἀφανίσθητε
324+80   +1361   +31   +957 +31   +1084
        = 3868.

This is Ἰησοῦς Χριστὸς 2368+φῶς 1500   = 3868

"For I will work a work in your days"

Ὅτι ἔργον ἐργάζομαι ἐγὼ ἐν ταῖς ἡμέραις ὑμῶν.
380 +228   +237 +808+55+511+264+1290
        = 3773.

μέγα φῶς ἡ παρουσία τοῦ Θεοῦ.   3773

"Righteousness: the Authority of the Lord God."

Δικαιοσύνη · ἐξουσία τοῦ Θεοῦ Κυρίου.
        773   3000   = 3773.

"Which ye will not believe"

ἔργον ᾧ οὐ μὴ πιστεύσητε.

228 + 800 + 470 + 48 + 1508   = 3054.

This is ἀνάστασις σαρκὸς, 1554 + φῶς = 3054

"If one declare it unto you"

ἐάν τις ἐκδιηγῆται ὑμῖν   1435

56 + 510 + 369 + 500 = 1435   ——

                                                    4489

which is "Authority of Michael"

ἐξουσία Μιχαήλ   1435

the whole number giving :—

"Light of the World : Salvation of the Lord"

φῶς κόσμου · σωτηρία τοῦ κυρίου.   4489

The Light of the Salvation of the Lord

Τὸ φῶς σωτηρίας κυρίου.   4489

Ἰησοῦς · ὁ ἅγιος Ἰσραήλ · ὁ λόγος Κυρίου · ὁ ἄγγελος

                                                    4489

Ἰησοῦς Χριστὸς · τὸ Ἄλφα · ὁ λόγος ἐκ πατρός

Χριστὸς ὁ ἄγγελος σωτήρ · ὁ λόγος ἐκ πατρός

                                    (I.X. Θ. Υ. Σ.)

This is certainly a strange combination. There is first the Light of Christ. Then there is the inner meaning of the teaching of the Light. Then the rising again to Light coupled apparently with the name of one who is always in Christian art, at least, closely connected with the Resurrection Day. It was a warning in the spirit and language of the prophets.

These examples will show some of the difficulties and also, we trust, will show that they are not insuperable.

THE TEMPTATION IN THE WILDERNESS.

PRELIMINARY NOTE.

St. Matthew iv, 1—11 differs from St. Luke iv, 1—13
in certain particulars of no apparent importance to the
general understanding of the story, but which will certainly affect any attempt to show the presence of
gematria, and even to some slight extent affect interpretation. Those features that will be dealt with here
are the following.

St. Matthew uses the plural "these stones," St. Luke
the singular "this stone." If there is any real distinc-
tion, which is doubtful, the single stone would seem
a more immediate and personal temptation while the
larger number would indicate a more public and popular
use of the power in feeding multitudes. In the answer,
the words "Man shall not live by bread alone" are
common to both accounts, but the second clause is probably to be omitted in St. Luke, and does not exactly
follow the Septuagint in St. Matthew.

The second and third temptations are transposed in
St. Luke, which makes it doubtful what was the actual
or the symbolical order in which the temptations were
presented. On this point much could be written, but it
will suffice to adopt provisionally St. Matthew's order
and to state briefly that the Galileans would follow for
loaves, Jerusalem would accept a sign from heaven, and
lastly that the whole power of the Roman Empire was
at the service of a worshipper of the devil; also that
the suggestions were plausible. For the temptations,
to be temptations, must be real, and not such as to be
rejected as a matter of course, as in "Paradise Regained."
Perhaps it is not too much to say that they are still
the temptations of every prophet, seer or reformer, and,
if yielded to, bring temporary success at most, and
certain spiritual failure at the end.

The Lord therefore meets them and repels them at the very outset of His ministry, during which they recur to Him again and again, for the devil only departed from Him "for a season." The present object is to study the form they took.

THE TEMPTATIONS.
A Study in Gematria.

The first temptation of our Lord mentioned in St. Matthew iv. shows a remarkable adherence to the "metacubic" law which we have found to govern the names, titles, and epithets of Jesus Christ.

Thus the words in the mouth of Satan are made, as it were unconsciously to testify to the reality of the majesty of Him whom the tempter was addressing. Thus we find:—

"If Thou be the Son of God

Εἰ υἱὸς εἶ τοῦ Θεοῦ $= 1964 = $ Χριστὸς Θεοῦ.

command that (these) stones

εἰπὲ ἵνα οἱ λίθοι $= 370$

(these) be made bread

οὗτοι ἄρτοι γένωνται $= 2550$

$$4884 = 37 \times 132,$$

$$\begin{cases} \text{Χριστὸς ὁ Λόγος Κυ-} \\ \text{ρίου ὁ Μεσσίας} \\ \text{Θεοῦ Πατρός,} \end{cases}$$

or Ἰησοῦς Χριστός · Ἐξουσία τοῦ Κυρίου.

Now the concealed teaching here may be explored a great deal further, for

Εἰ Ὑιὸς εἶ $= 710 = $ Ἅγιον πνεῦμα,

so that εἰ υἱὸς εἶ τοῦ Θεοῦ $= $ Χριστὸς Θεοῦ, and Ἅγιον Πνεῦμα τοῦ Θεοῦ,

and it is also $= $ Ὁ Λόγος τοῦ Πατρός.

Ὁ οὖκος ἀχειροποίητος.

Ἡ Ζωὴ αἰώνιος.

and what are οἱ λίθοι οὗτοι ... 1059 but the mysteries (μυστήρια) 1059 in which may be made manifest the power of the Fatherhood (πατρότης) 1059, of the Fulness (πλήρωμα) 1059 and the Great Paraclete (μέγας παράκλητος) 1059.

The concluding words are significant.

$$\text{Ἄρτοι, } 481 = \text{Loaves,}$$
$$\text{Γένωνται, } 1219 = \text{Fish (ἰχθὺς).}$$

As in the farewell word ἔῤῥωσθε we may discern the Christian pass-word, so in this narrative, the last word may be held to convey the message of truth to the disciple of the Faith.

We have no space here to give even an outline of the wonderful richness of the gematria of the number 4884, perhaps unsurpassed in the fulness of the choice of sovereign titles of Christ by any of the multiples of the sacred geometric 37. The two specimens we have given above must suffice.

Let us pass, then, to the answer made by Jesus to the devil. This answer should be an affirmation of the truth so unwillingly uttered by the adversary, and if our theory of the gematria hold good, we shall hope to find equally in this a record of the sacred geometry, the very Form of God in human words used by the Master.

Jesus says in reply:—
"Not by bread

οὐκ ἐπ᾽ ἄρτῳ   1776 $= \mathring{η}$ χάρις · λόγος Θεοῦ
$$(2 \times 888).$$
Grace, the Word of God.

alone

μόνῳ   960

————2736 = ὁ σωτὴρ ὁ λειτουργός.
The Saviour, the Minister.

shall Man live,

ζήσεται ὁ ἄνθρωπος   1911 = χάρις Κυρίου.

$$4647 = \text{'Ιησοῦς Χριστὸς κατὰ μυ-}$$
στήριον ὑπακόης.

Jesus Christ according to the mystery of obedience.

but by every word proceeding

ἀλλ' ἐπὶ παντὶ ῥήματι ἐκπο-
ρευομένῳ   2701   = 37 × 73 = ὁ λειτουργός · ὁ λόγος Κυρίου.

from the mouth of God"

διὰ στόματος Θεοῦ 1680   = Χριστοῦ (of Christ).

———4381

$$9028 = 37 \times 244 = 4844 + 4144.$$

So Jesus answers Satan by another of the sacred numbers, in which lie hidden yet higher and more complex values of the mystery of Messiahship. For to the Devil's 4884 he adds 4144 and in this we find the nature of the addition He makes. For 4144 (37 × 112, or 37 × 7 × 16) stands for

Σταυρὸς Κύριου · Λόγος κατὰ μυστήριον.

Ἡ γνῶσις Κυρίου · Λόγος κατὰ μυστήριον.

Ἡ δύναμις φωνῆς · Λόγος κατὰ μυστήριον.

Ἡ ζῶσα φωνὴ τοῦ Κύριου.

Ἡ φωνὴ ἡ μεγάλη ἐκ τῶν οὐρανῶν.

Ἰησοῦς Χριστὸς ὁ ἅγιος Ἰσραήλ. (2368 + 1776.)

The total 9028 symbolically portrays the controversy of Satan against Jesus Christ.

For 9208 = 2368 = Ἰησοῦς Χριστὸς.

plus   6660 = Number of the Adversary or Anti-Christ raised tenfold.

———

9028

And lastly, as evidence of the extraordinary perfection of the geometry interwoven with the gematria of the challenge and the reply, we have this

Challenge $= 37 \times 132$

Reply $\quad = 37 \times 244$ and $\dfrac{244}{132} = 1\cdot8485$.

This fraction expresses the mystery of the A.Ω. in the geometric relation $1 : 8\cdot485$ (see *Preliminary Investigation*, p. 42 *f*).

Reply $\quad = 37 \times 244$
Challenge $= 37 \times 132$
————
Difference $= 37 \times 112$ and $\dfrac{132}{112} = 1\cdot1785 = \mathrm{M}\upsilon\sigma\tau\acute{\eta}\rho\iota o\nu \times 10.$

This fraction perfectly expresses to five places of decimals the volume of the Tetrahedron (Alpha) whose edge $= 1$ ($\cdot11785$). $8\cdot485$ and $\cdot11785$ are both "functions" of the mathematical root of Two ($\sqrt{2}$), always typical of Divine order in creation.

The Creative Unit (Root 2) is typically divided by six and restored to a higher symmetry by a fivefold multiplication, even as the Tetrahedron whose mathematical symbol is $\cdot11785$ is raised, in the Penterema, to a yet higher space and appears as a transcendental figure in our teaching—the mystical Five Words appearing on the Lord's Robe of Light (Pistis Sophia).

They are reciprocal numbers indicating the One-ness of the A and Ω mysteries, as the Pistis Sophia says.

For A ($\mu\upsilon\sigma\tau\acute{\eta}\rho\iota o\nu$) $= 1178$
and $\quad \Omega\mu\epsilon\gamma\alpha \quad = 849$
and $1000 \div \cdot1178 \quad = 849.$

THE SECOND TEMPTATION.

Again in this Temptation we have

Εἰ Ὑιὸς εἶ τοῦ Θεοῦ = Χριστὸς Θεοῦ, or Ἅγιον πνεῦμα τοῦ
$$\text{Θεοῦ,}$$
$$= 1964$$
with the addition

"cast Thyself down"

βάλε σεαυτόν κάτω = 2185 = ὁ αἰὼν τοῦ Θεοῦ (Χριστὸς +
δύναμις).

4149 = Ἰησοῦς Χριστὸς Κύριος
σοφίας,
Λόγος τοῦ Κυρίου · Πνεῦμα
ἐξουσίας Θεοῦ.
Λόγος ἐκ Θεοῦ πατρός ·
Ἐξουσία τοῦ Κυρίου.
Ὁ ζῶν λόγος · Μόνος Κύριος
σωτηρίας.
Κύριος τοῦ αἰῶνος · Ὁ μονο-
γενὴς Λόγος ἐκ Θεοῦ.
Ἰησοῦς Χριστὸς Θεὸς · Ἐξου-
σία Πατρός.

But 4149 also = Ῥώμη, 666. Μυστήριον τοῦ Διαβόλου.
Μυστήριον Ῥώμης · ὁ ἀριθμὸς τοῦ Σατανᾶ.

The rest of Satan's speech must be left for further research, as it runs into very high numbers, and the inclusion of the Ὅτι is debateable, as also the ν ἐφελκυστικὸν in ἄρουσι (ν).

But the answer of Jesus is

"Thou shalt not tempt the Lord thy God"

Οὐκ ἐκπειράσεις Κύριον 1776 = Ἡ σωτηρία Ἰσραήλ (a
double 888).

τὸν Θεὸν σοῦ 1224 = ὁ Κύριος ὁ Θεός.

3000 = Ἐξουσία τοῦ Θεοῦ Κυρίου.

THE THIRD TEMPTATION.

Similarly with the third Temptation, we must defer a complete analysis until these high numbers have been further explored, for it is not within the power of individual workers to attain complete results.

This, the final Temptation, in St. Matthew's order, was a vision rather than a speech. And if there is any gematria, it must be looked for in the words "All these things will I give Thee, if Thou wilt fall down and worship me."

Ταῦτα πάντα σοι δώσω ἐὰν πεσὼν προσκυνήσῃς μοι.
1002 +432+280+1804+56+1135 +1336 +120
= 6165.

This is a very large number, and its interpretation is therefore highly speculative. But a very striking hint was arrived at thus : A high multiple of 37 subtracted from a large number may leave a significant difference. In this case the number 5217 (37 × 141) which will stand for Ἰησοῦς Χριστὸς ὁ Θεὸς τῶν Ἰουδαίων left the difference 948 which is the number of Ῥώμη.

But it is a very different matter when we come to the answer. Whatever "Gnosis falsely so called" more or less corresponding to the true may be found in the temptations of the devil, never was the Sword of the Spirit, which is the Word of God wielded with more life and energy than here. Quick and powerful, sharper than any two edged sword, it discerned the matter and showed to whom the worship was due.

"Thou shalt worship the Lord thy God."
Κύριον τὸν Θεόν σου προσκυνήσεις.
650+420+134+670 +1343   = 3217
"And Him only shalt thou serve."
Καὶ αὐτῷ μόνῳ λατρεύσεις.
31+1501+960 +1251   = 3743
—————
6960

Ιησοῦς Χριστὸς ἡ Μονὰς ἐν Τριάδι.   3217
Jesus Christ the One in Three.

Λόγος τοῦ Κυρίου · Κύριος κόσμου.   3743
Word of the Lord : Lord of the Universe.

Ὕπαρξις Κυρίου · Ὁ Παντοκράτωρ.   3743
Substance of the Lord : Omnipotent.

for the total we may read $2960 + 4000 = 6960$

    = Ὑιὸς τοῦ ἀνθρώπου · φῶς Κυρίου κατὰ μυστήριον.
    Son of Man : Light of the Lord according to the
    Mystery.

Note on 6165. It has been suggested that the notation
of this number may be chosen as implying the 666 of
the "Beast" (*i.e.* $6+6+1$ and 5). For the appreciation
of those of our readers who may be inclined to speculate
on the possible implications contained in the 6165, we
give the following purely empirical combinations but
without attaching any weight to them.

6165

Ταῦτα πάντα σοι δώσω ἐὰν πεσὼν
προσκυνήσῃς μοι—" All these things will I
                give Thee if Thou wilt
                fall down and worship me "

for which we may read : if we will

Ὁ Σατανᾶς · Λεγέων Δαιμονίων · Κύριος Ῥώμης ·
    Εὐπορία κόσμου.
Satan : Legion of Devils : Lord of Rome : Wealth of
    the World (or Material Wealth).

    (Note εὐπορία is the only noun in the New
        Testament having the number 666, excepting
        ὁ σπείρας.)

Ἡ Ῥώμη · Δύναμις τοῦ κόσμου καὶ κυριεία τοῦ κύριου
    διαβόλου.
= Rome : Power of the World and Dominion of the
    Lord the Devil.

Ἡ μεγάλη πόλις · Ἡ κυριότης ὑπὲρ τὴν εὐπορίαν · τό μυστήριον τοῦ διαβόλου.

The Great City : the Dominion over Wealth : Mystery of the Devil.

To sum up the conclusion of the whole matter. All three answers of the Lord as given in St. Matthew, and checked against St. Luke, are susceptible of interpretation by an orthodox and congruous gematria. There is strong indication of gematria in the Temptations as offered by the Devil. If a choice must be made, though it is hazardous to make a choice at this stage, it would be that St. Matthew is probably the better authority, as being an apostle and an eye-witness of the Lord's ministry, who heard the teaching at first hand. But none can say that St. Luke is very far from the truth.

THE MIRACLES.

ST. MARK.

Μάρκος μὲν ἑρμηνευτὴς Πέτρου γενόμενος, ὅσα ἐμνημόνευσεν ἀκριβῶς ἔγραψεν. Eusebius iii cap : ult : "Mark became the interpreter of Peter and wrote accurately whatever he remembered." See Routh, Reliquiæ Sacræ, I, 13.

Such is the brief but valuable hint given concerning this Gospel of St. Mark, which seems to contain, on the whole, more of the words that accompanied our Lord's miracles than the other Gospels.

The plan adopted here is to take the miracles in order as they are narrated by St. Mark and to append those from the other Gospels and the Acts.

As little comment as possible will be added.

THE DEVIL IN THE SYNAGOGUE.
St. Mark i, 21 *sqq.*

The first recorded miracle here is the casting out of a devil who cried aloud in the synagogue from a man's mouth. The evangelist has just mentioned that the Lord taught as one having ἐξουσία and this word will be found freely in the examples that follow.

The cry of the devil was suppressed instantly.

Φιμώθητι καὶ ἔξελθε ἐξ αὐτοῦ.
    1677 + 31 + 114 + 65 + 1171 = 3058.
on which we find

Μυστήριον Υἱοῦ Κυρίου
Θεότης Κύριος ἐνσώματος
Δύναμις ἐξουσίας, ἡ Κληρονομία Κυρίου.
Ὁ αἰὼν τῆς σωτηρίας.
ΑΩ · Ἀμήν · Ὁ Υἱὸς Σωτήρ.
Εὐαγγέλιον Κυρίου, Δύναμις ἐκ Πατρός.

Our Lord did not suffer the devils to speak for they
knew that He was Christ. He did not need such
testimony, and on occasion a lie might be hidden in
the truth they told. The Revised Text omits Χριστὸν
εἶναι in v. 34. The words are not really needed for the
sense.

It is clear that in this case there was something very
dangerous. It is obvious that in the Synoptics the
Messiahship or Christ-hood of the Lord was at first to
be kept a secret. "He charged them that they should
tell no man that He was the Christ." But in the
Gospel according to St. John there is no secret from
the very first. And of all persons to whom a secret
would not be entrusted, the village gossip at the
Samaritan well-head would be the most typical. Yet
she was told, and told others, and the gematria of
Ἐγὼ εἰμι ὁ λάλων σοῖ = 2134 = Μεσσίας ὁ σωτήρ. The
only explanation apparent is that St. John, writing so
very late as he did, had forgotten that there ever had
been a secret, and only remembered the early inti-
mations of which the Spirit revealed the meaning
subsequently. But we admit that this is not very
satisfactory.

The problem of the need of a witness at the trial
before Caiaphas intrudes itself. Two were required by
the law, and Judas was the only one. But our present
concern is with this devil, whose words are Τί ἡμῖν καὶ
σοί, Ἰησοῦ Ναζαρηνέ; ἦλθες ἀπολέσαι ἡμᾶς; οἶδά σε τίς
εἶ, ὁ ἅγιος τοῦ Θεοῦ. This adds up to 4960, which might
have a good import (*e.g.* Ὑιὸς τοῦ ἀνθρώπου, ἐξουσία τοῦ
Θεοῦ 4960) though a very sinister meaning could be
attached to it. For 4960 is the sum of the two
numbers :—

In St. Luke iv, 35, the reading ἀπ' for ἐξ gives
3064 = πλήρωμα τοῦ Θεοῦ πατρός.

2214
2746
———
4960

2214 has already (Part I, p. 50) been shown as
'Η θεότης 'Ρώμη χξϛ'
while 2746 is ὡς ἐξουσία Κυρίου.

The two together representing a power of seemingly invincible might in antagonism to a power it dreaded.

And if such an idea were propounded and propagated the temptation of the wilderness would come on our Lord again with tremendous force, for unless He could seize the kingdoms of the world the power of the world would seem certain to overwhelm Him. No one would accept such an interpretation of 4960 as

'Ιησοῦς Χριστὸς	2368
ὁ Λόγος	443
	———2811
ἡ χάρις	919
ἀφίεναι ἁμαρτίας	1230
	———2149
	4960

Though presently we shall show what ἡ χάρις Κυρίου 'Ιησοῦ Χριστοῦ could do with a devil, and it is clear that we have a straightforward interpretation of the Divine implication of this sentence in

Jesus Christ, Godhead, Authority of God.
'Ιησοῦς Χριστὸς θεότης · ἐξουσία τοῦ Θεοῦ.
888 +1480 +592 +746+770+484=4960.

The healing of St. Peter's wife's mother is not accompanied by any words, and, the next miracle where the words are given is the cleansing of the leper, v. 40.

THE LEPER.

The prayer of the leper was in its terms a double
one.   His disease was both an actual and a ceremonial
disqualification.   There seems nothing discoverable in
the number 1371 which is the total of ἐὰν θέλῃς δύνασαί
με καθαρίσαι. "If thou wilt thou canst make me clean."
But the answer is very significant, identical in three
gospels.

Θέλω · Καθαρίσθητι.   (I will: be thou clean)   = 1512
  844   668

Both powers are there :

'Ο Μεσσίας   726
'Η ἐκκλησία Θεοῦ   786
                                 ─────
                                 1512

Which is also

'Ο λόγος ἀγάπης ἐκ Πατρὸς,   1512
Πᾶσα ἐξουσία Θεοῦ,   1512
and very mystically
'Ο νόμος Μελχισεδέκ · 'Αγάπη,   1512.

Whether there is anything more than appears exote-
rically in the parting directions to the cleansed leper
seems difficult to decide.   Psychologically the confirmation
of the cure by the priest would strengthen the belief
in the man that his cure was real, and ecclesiastically the
priest's certificate would readmit him to the congregation.
And perhaps this was quite enough to expect, especially
as the words differ in the three accounts.   Nevertheless
the countings may be given thus. "Ορα μηδενὶ μηδὲν
εἴπῃς, ἀλλ' ὕπαγε σεαυτὸν δεῖξον τῷ ἱερεῖ = 3703. "See
that thou tell no man anything, but go thy way, show
thyself to the priest."   Καὶ προσένεγκε περὶ τοῦ καθαρι-
σμοῦ σοῦ = 3055. "And offer concerning thy cleansing."
ᵃΑ προσέταξε Μῶσης εἰς μαρτύριον αὐτοῖς = 4337. "That
which Moses commanded as a witness to them."

No certain interpretation can be suggested, for any of these three numbers, 3703, 3055, 4337, which may be, after all, a wrong division of the text. But the probability is strong that there is no gematria here.

St. Matthew viii, 1—4: St. Luke v, 12—16.

THE SICK OF THE PALSY.

St. Mark ii, 1—12.

The next miracle is extremely important and will again be referred to as connecting the Gnosis with the forgiveness of sins.

The first words spoken to the sick of the palsy are " Son, thy sins are forgiven." But there are two notable variants in the reading. The Revisers read

Τέκνον	495
ἀφέωνταί	1667
σου	670
ἁι	11
ἁμαρτίαι	463
	3306

This will stand for ἐξουσία Ὑιοῦ Χριστοῦ = Authority of Christ the Son,—which was exactly that claimed. And if ἀφίενται is read the number becomes 2516 (37 × 68), which is

The Authority of the Lord.

Ἐξουσία τοῦ Κυρίου.

2516 is also

Ἅγιον μυστήριον Βαπτίσματος.

Ἡ δύναμις Λόγου ἀφίεναι ἁμαρτίας.

Μεγάλη δύναμις ἐκκλησίας ἀφίεναι ἁμαρτίας,

which will stand for ἐξουσία τοῦ Κυρίου, with little difference.

"'Aφέωνται is a very difficult word about which the old grammarians were very much divided." It seems to be a perf. subj. passive.

(See Alford, or any good commentary.)

The addition of σοῖ making "Son, thy sins are forgiven thee" will give 3306 + 280 = 3586 = 2178 + 1408 or μυστήριον Κυρίου added to Σωτήρ, or μυστήριον· μυστήριον ἀφίεναι ἁμαρτίας. All the readings therefore have some claim to respect.

The final word in the Revisers' reading and spelling is : Σοὶ λέγω, ἔγειραι, ἆρον τὸν κράββατόν σοῦ καὶ ὕπαγε εἰς τὸν οἶκόν σου. 5154 with the wonderful gematria combining both the mystery of the Lord and the authority of the Lord with the forgiveness of sins, 2178 + 1746 + 577 (ἀφίεναι) + 653 (ἁμαρτίας) = 5154.

Ἰησοῦς Χριστὸς ὁ Ὑιὸς, ἡ πᾶσα ἐξουσία Κυρίου   5154
Ἡ γεωμετρία· ἐξουσία τοῦ Ἰησοῦ σωτῆρος   5154

This number 2178 will also stand for ἡ μετάθεσις τοῦ νόμου, the changing of the law, mentioned or hinted at in the Epistle to the Hebrews.

St. Matthew ix, i—8; St. Luke v, 17—26.

THE WITHERED HAND.

St. Mark iii, 16; St. Luke vi, 6; St. Matthew xii, 9.

The miracle of a man with the withered hand has another subject. Jesus Christ is Lord of the Sabbath, and can act as He will thereon. There is a crowd of hostile theologians ready with a syllogism.

No work must be done on the Sabbath.
Healing is work.
No healing must be done on the Sabbath.

For saner views on syllogistic logic read the "Novum Organon" by Francis Bacon.

But the theologians were given their chance.

"Arise into the midst," said the Lord.

Ἔγειραι εἰς τὸ μέσον.

134+215+370 +365 = 1084.

The Lord God gives this order. Κύριος Θεός, 1084. St. Luke adds the words καὶ στῆθι before εἰς τὸ μέσον. The total then is 1642 which is much the same, as it is Φωνή+Θεός = 1358+284 = 1642. St. Matthew omits this order. This number is recorded as an ancient Gnostic number relating to Christ as Μονὰς πάντων.

But all agree to the word that healed

Ἔκτεινον τὴν χεῖρά σου.

510 + 358 + 716 + 670 = 2254.

This may be ἡ ἐξουσία + φῶς = 2254,

or δύναμις + μέγα φῶς = 2254.

705   1549

1549 is a great number in the Gnosis.

The total of these numbers 1084+2254 is 3338 and may represent "The true learning of the Lord of the Sabbath."

Ἡ ἀληθινὴ μάθησις Κυρίου τοῦ σαββάτου.

8 +116 +468 +1000+770 +976 = 3338.

Or again :—

The grace of the Lord, salvation.

Ἡ χάρις Κυρίου, σωτηρία   3338.

The living Church, all power of the Lord.

Ἡ ἐκκλησία ζῶσα, πᾶσα ἐξουσία Κυρίου   3338.

Ἡ σοφία · τὸ Α' μυστήριον Κυρίου   3338.

The addition in St. Luke gives no discoverable gematria here.

THE TESTIMONY OF THE DEVILS.

St. Mark iii, 11 and 22.

In this chapter St. Mark records yet another testimony of the unclean spirits frequently given as they came out.

"Thou art the Son of God."

Σὺ εἶ ὁ υἱὸς τοῦ Θεοῦ.

$600 + 15 + 70 + 680 + 770 + 484 = 2619.$

This likewise was constantly rebuked.

It will stand for:

Σημεῖον · Τὸ μυστήριον Ἰησοῦ.

$383 + 370 + 1178 + 688.$

But this can also be read

Τὸ σημεῖον · μυστήριον Ἰησοῦ.

But τὸ σημεῖον $= 753$ is also Σατανᾶς $= 753$. So that the whole as far as the gematria is concerned would, in the mouth of devils, very clearly imply the blasphemy.

Σατανᾶς μυστήριον Ἰησοῦ,

or

Ἰησοῦς μυστήριον Σατανᾶ,

and hence merit the rebuke.

The next paragraph records the mission and names of the Apostles, and then follows a very important passage which has greatly and needlessly distressed so many servants of the Lord. The context is this: Our Lord's friends think Him mad. His enemies make a blasphemous suggestion which is apparently founded on this testimony of the unclean spirits, and which brings down a tremendous condemnation. Can it be that the Lord's enemies had any acquaintance with the "morphosis" (see Rom. ii, 20) of the gematria? That is a question that may be asked from the point of view of this research. The implication is affirmative. Without entering on the question of the origin of evil, the gematria shows a conjunction of two names, Jesus and Satan. Clearly the latter is subordinate, as the exoteric confession, "Thou art the Son of God," (ὁ υἱὸς) shows. According to the Book of Job Satan is among the sons of God, and consequently in subjection to the Son. But to invert this testimony wilfully and maliciously is desperate, hopeless blasphemy.

And to use the name of the base Ekronite god instead of the dignified and serious name Satan was to add a sneer to the blasphemy.

Satan cannot cast out Satan. The devils were cast out both by the Lord and by the sons of His enemies by "the finger of God." (See St. Luke xi, 15.) Whether such an account of the passage as is here put forth is adequate may be open to question, but there is matter for grave consideration.

Was it by the suggestion of a devil that the enemies of the Lord were tempted to commit the sin that hath never forgiveness?

STILLING THE STORM.
St. Mark iv, 39.

The next miracle in which a word is used is where the stormy sea is stilled. This comes naturally as a sequel to the parables which are most fully dealt with in St. Matthew. St. Mark alone gives the words Σιώπα· πεφίμωσο but to these it would seem that Ἡ θάλασσα should be prefixed. (See Vol. I, p. 112.) This would be the articular nominative used as a vocative and about this there is more to say (see p. 43).

The result is Ἰησοῦς φωνὴ Κυρίου 3246 888 + 1358 + 1000, and φωνὴ Κυρίου is also τὸ πλοῖον σωτῆρος and πᾶς γραμματεὺς μαθητευθείς, and φῶς ἐξουσία Κυρίου is also 3246.

The wind would have made the voice of command inaudible, but He arose and with a gesture rebuked it. Then He spake to the sea and the sea sank to a calm. St. Peter then heard the words. St. Mark wrote them from St. Peter's mouth.

3246 is also 1746 + 1500. Κόκκος σινάπεως + φῶς, or Λόγος Κυρίου Λόγος δυνάμεως.

THE LEGION OF DEVILS.
St. Mark v, 8.

The shore being reached there rushed to meet the boat the most terrible demoniac yet encountered. No one was present save the disciples and the Lord; and therefore, it would seem, the devil was allowed to speak even after the word that must be obeyed had gone forth.

"Come out of the Man, thou unclean spirit."

Ἔξελθε τὸ πνεῦμα τὸ ἀκάθαρτον ἐκ τοῦ ἀνθρώπου.

$$114+370+576+370 \quad +552 +25+770 +1510$$
$$=4287.$$

The interpretation is plain

Ἡ Χάρις	919
Κύριου	1000
Ἰησοῦ Χριστοῦ	2368
	4287

It may also be φωνή · πλήρωμα φωτός, and φῶς ἡ πᾶσα ἐξουσία Κυρίου πατρός. 4287.

It has been already mentioned that a danger lurked in the number 2214 representing

"My name is Legion, for we are many."

Λεγεὼν ὄνομά μοι, ὅτι πολλοί ἐσμεν,

which is the number of Σατανᾶς Ἀπολλύων and Ἡ θεότης Ῥώμη χξϛ' (see p. 31), and this danger is further indicated when ἀγέλη χοίρων μεγάλη βοσκομένη, a great herd of swine feeding, can be interpreted as 2229 = ὁ λεγεὼν · ἡ θεοτὴς χξϛ'. But this mystery has not been fully worked out yet, and from its historical importance will need great care.

St. Mark v, 21.

The raising of the daughter of Jairus is accompanied in all three Synoptics by the miracle that took place on the way, the healing of the woman with the issue of blood. No word is spoken until the miracle is performed, but the woman's faith sufficed and the words are simply confirmatory. The three accounts differ verbally, but taking St. Mark as the standard we have first of all the Lord's question, " Who touched my clothes ? "

Τίς μου ἥψατο τῶν ἱματίων.
510+510+1079+1150+1211 = 4460.

This is Ὑιὸς τοῦ ἀνθρώπου, { 2960
κατὰ μυστήριον { 1500
which has several interpretations, all to the point. It is also

Μυστήριον Κυρίου, πᾶσα ἐξουσία τοῦ Θεοῦ. 4460
Τὸ φῶς, ἐκπόρευσις δυνάμεως. 4460

St. Matthew omits this. St. Luke gives
Τίς ὁ ἁψάμενός μου ; 2157
which may be Θεὸς + Λόγος + κατὰ μυστήριον. 2157

But the existence of gematria is rather doubtful in the words that St. Luke gives ; St. Mark being content to say " Jesus knowing in himself that virtue had gone out of Him." And the words in St. Luke are addressed to the disciples.

But the final blessing, as given by St. Mark, is very noteworthy. " Daughter, thy faith has saved thee, go in peace and be whole of thy plague."

Θύγατερ, ἡ πίστις σου σέσωκέ σε ὕπαγε εἰς εἰρήνην.
818 +8 +800+670+1230+205+489+215+231
= 4666.

This total will stand for Κύριος Ἰησοῦς ὁ Σωτὴρ with φῶς added 4666

And part of it may be compared with the words spoken to Bartimaeus.

Ἡ πίστις σου = 1478 = ὁ Σωτήρ, and σέσωκέ σε = 1435 = Βάπτισμα + περιστέρα.

And the last words

Καὶ ἴσθι ὑγιὴς ἀπὸ τῆς μάστιγός σου.

$31+229+621+151+508 \quad +824 \quad +670 \qquad =3034$

which is 37×82 and has on it

Κύριος Θεὸς ὁ ὕψιστος,	3034
Ὁ Χριστὸς Θεοῦ Κυρίου,	3034
Λόγος πατρὸς, Μεσσίας τοῦ Θεοῦ,	3034
Χριστὸς ἀνάστασις σαρκὸς,	3034

THE RAISING OF JAIRUS' DAUGHTER.

After this miracle the message comes that the girl is dead and that the Lord need not be further troubled ; but this evokes the answer given by St. Mark as " Be not afraid only believe," to which St. Luke adds " and she shall be saved."

Μὴ φοβοῦ μόνον πίστευε.

$48 +1042+280 +1000 \qquad =2370$

which gives :

Ὁ Κύριος κατὰ μυστήριον	$=2370$
Ὁ Κύριος + φῶς	$=2370$

If καὶ σωθήσεται, 1564, be added, the result $2370+1564 = 3934$, gives this

Ἐξουσία Κυρίου φῶς Ἰησοῦ,	3934
φῶς ἐξουσία Κυρίου Ἰησοῦ,	3934.

Note that ἐξουσία Κυρίου 1746 = Κόκκος σινάπεως.

Then the house is reached, where the professional mourners are already at their task and must be dismissed before an atmosphere of faith can be secured.

Here in the three accounts there is divergence in the actual words. And this must be taken account of because here and elsewhere where the same thing occurs questions can be asked to which no answer can be given without committing the answerer to a theory of some sort. But the facts seem fairly clear. St. Luke was certainly not an eye-witness, but like the good historian

he is, he tells us who were, thereby excluding St. Matthew;
but, admitting that St. Peter speaks through St. Mark,
St. Mark's is the account of the eye-witness, but St.
Matthew was very near. St. Mark gives the following:
"Why make ye this ado and weep? the damsel is not
dead but sleepeth."

Τί   θορυβεῖσθε καὶ κλαίετε ; τὸ παιδίον οὐκ ἀπέθανεν
310   +810 +31   +371+370 +225+490   +201
ἀλλὰ καθεύδει.
+62 +454   = 3324.

Which gives the following

Ἀνάστασις σαρκός τοῦ Κυρίου.   = 3324.
Δύναμις σωτηρίας Κυρίου.   = 3324.
Ἡ Θεότης, ἡ πᾶσα ἐξουσία Κυρίου Ἰησοῦ.   = 3324.
Τὸ μυστήριον, ἡ σωτηρία Ἰσραήλ.   = 3324.
Μυστήριον, ἡ ἐντὸς βασιλεία τοῦ Θεοῦ.   = 3324.

In St. Matthew ix, 24 the words are, "Give place for
the maid is not dead but sleepeth."

Ἀναχωρεῖτε, οὐ γὰρ ἀπέθανε τὸ κοράσιον ἀλλὰ καθεύδει.
1872 +470+104+151+370+521   +62 +454
= 4004.

This number will give,

Τὸ σημεῖον · Κύριος Χριστὸς ἡ ἀνάστασις.   = 4004.
Ἀνάστασις σαρκὸς τοῦ Χριστοῦ.   = 4004.

interpretations which closely correspond with those to
St. Mark's version.

On the other hand St. Luke's version, Revisers' text,
Μὴ κλαίετε οὐ γὰρ ἀπέθανεν ἀλλὰ καθεύδει, counting at
1710 appears to have no significant gematria here. But
if the reading be οὐκ instead of οὐ γὰρ, the number is
1626 and gives ἐξουσία υἱοῦ = 1626.

When the room was clear and only faithful people
present the Lord raised the dead child to life.

St. Matthew gives no word as spoken, but he uses the
words τὸ κοράσιον with the passive ἠγέρθη.

St. Mark gives the words in transliterated aramaic.

Ταλιθά, κοῦμι,   891,

which is the same number as

Τὸ κοράσιον,   891.

St. Luke gives,

'Η παῖς ἐγείρου.

8+291+593   = 892.

The Revisers read ἐγείρου instead of the usual ἔγειραι or ἔγειρε.

But St. Mark gives an interpretation,

Τὸ κοράσιον σοὶ λέγω, ἔγειραι.

891   +280+838 +134   =2143

which gives

Λόγος τοῦ Κυρίου   =2143

and is also the sum of 919+484+740=2143.

919 is Μελχισεδέκ, or ἡ χάρις.   See the Ep. Hebrews.

484 is Θεοῦ, of God.

740 half 1480 or Χριστὸς, and will stand for παρθὲνος +παιδίον.

With regard to the numbers 891 and 892, with which 890 may also be associated there is room for a large amount of conjecture but at present no certainty to which credence can be unhesitatingly given.

890 is   Ὄλυμπος
      and Ἔναυλον Διός.

891 is Οὐρανός,
      also which might be relevant here, ὁ Λόγος ὁ ἀληθινός.

892 is a nearer approximation to a rough proportional representing π.

If 284 Θεὸς be the diameter, the circumference is about 892—actually 892·5, and on 891 we have

Οἱ ἄστερες. The Stars.

Οὐρανία Βασιλεία. Heavenly Kingdom.

Ὁ κυριακος. The Church.

Ἡ κληρονομία Θεοῦ. The inheritance of God.

And 892 is a number of the Saros or lunar calculus of 223 limations. On this the prophetic numbers in the prophet Daniel are regarded as based. And 891 would be an alternative calculus.

The use of the articular nominative as a vocative Ἡ παῖς, and τὸ κοράσιον, should be noted. When our Lord addresses the spiritual world this is used often, *e.g.* τὸ πνεῦμα τὸ ἀκάθαρτον. See Moulton's Grammar of the New Testament, p. 70. He describes the earlier use of this in classical Greek as "rough and peremptory" in tone, but still recognises a "decisiveness" as surviving, but says that "descriptiveness" is rather the note of the articular nominative in the New Testament. Robertson (p. 465) criticises Moulton and does not seem to regard the use as significant to any noteworthy extent. But the voices that reached the dead or overawed the demons may well be regarded as peremptory and decisive, and when the two other cases of raising the dead are reached the question will come up again.

THE FEEDING OF THE FIVE THOUSAND.

St. Matthew xiv; St. Mark vi; St. Luke xvi; St. John vi.

Note by Dr. LEA.

The examples of Gematria given under the ensuing eight numbers, as well as in the further miracles will be found fewer than usual. For this departure from the canons tentatively adopted in this work I accept sole responsibility.

It can be shewn that where such high totals of enumeration are concerned, there must needs be Gematria on every number. The doctrine of chances is not eliminated.

But where we have eight consecutive numbers in as many sentences all bearing on one subject, I am of opinion that the rule which would hold for an isolated sentence may be relaxed. In each of these eight cases, the exoteric sense is eucharistic. So, in each case, is the Gematria. This can hardly be an accident, and is therefore presumably intentional.

We are still, however, a long way from certainty as to the exact 'morphosis' of the Gematria. There must have been some clue to the interpretations, and the phrases grouped upon the multiples of 37 appear to provide a basis for these, the completion of the numbers being made by the addition of certain characteristic numbers represented by words having a corresponding sense.

But the theoretical number of possible combinations of words—and words too of a *generally* appropriate import—is so large that it is easy to see how soon one might be lost in mazes of arithmetic without the guidance of some fixed rule or canon of construction. (See Appendix.)—T. S. L.

The Lord twice fed the multitudes who came into the wilderness to hear Him and this occasion is the most typical. The actual words used by Him at the blessing of the food are not given, but the connection with the Lord's Supper has always been understood by Christians and this is well borne out in the words recorded.

They have no need to depart.

Οὐ χρείαν ἔχουσιν ἀπελθεῖν.

$470 + 766 + 1335 + 190 = 2761.$

This number is $888 + 1873$, and the 1873 stands for the Λόγος κατὰ μυστήριον of the Bruce Codex—such is the title of that book. It is also

Ἰησοῦς συγκοινωνός. $= 2761.$

Ὁ Υἱὸς, κοινωνία Κυρίου. $= 2761.$

Ἰησοῦς ἡ πρόσφατος ὅδος. $= 2761.$

Τὸ καταπέτασμα, μυστήριον ἀληθείας.

$370 + 949 + 1178 + 264 = 2761.$

The "new way" and the "vail" will be remembered in the Epistle to the Hebrews.

It goes on :
  Give ye them to eat.
  Δότε αὐτοῖς ὑμεῖς φαγεῖν.
  379 +981 +655 +569   = 2584.

This gives 142 = μαννά + 2442 (37 × 66)
and   512 = τὸ μαννά + 2072 (37 × 56).

So that
  Μαννά, Ἰησοῦς ἀνάστασις σαρκός.   = 2584.
  Μαννά, Ἰησοῦς Μεσσίας ἡμῶν.   = 2584.
  Μαννά, Χριστὸς, ἡ θεία λειτουργία.   = 2584.
  Τὸ μαννά τοῦ Κυρίου, ἡ παραθήκη ἡ κάλη. = 2584.
  Τὸ μαννά τοῦ Κυρίου, ἡ ἐκκλησία.   = 2584.
also
  Μυστήριον, μόρφη Ἰησοῦ.   = 2584.
  Ἄρτος ζωῆς ἡμῶν.   = 2584.

Then comes the story of the disciples' doubt and the Lord's question, given by St. Mark, "How many loaves have ye, go and see."
  Πόσους ἄρτους ἔχετε ; ὑπάγετε ἴδετε.
  1020 + 1071 + 915   + 794 + 324   = 4124.

He himself knew what he would do, says St. John.
  Χριστὸς Ἐμμανουήλ, ἐξουσία τοῦ Θεοῦ. = 4124.
  Ἄρτοι τῆς κοινωνίας · Σημεῖον τῆς καινῆς διαθήκης Θεοῦ.
                            = 4124.
  Ὁ ἄρτος Ἰσραήλ, ὁ Χριστὸς Θεοῦ Κυρίου. = 4124.
  Ἄρτος Κυρίου, σύμβολον σαρκὸς Κυρίου. = 4124.
and about 24 others, all eucharistic, have been found.

The disciples say, Five and two fishes.
  Πέντε ἄρτοι καὶ δύο ἴχθυες.
  440 + 481 + 31 + 474 + 1224   = 2650.

Here is the mystery or sacrament.
  Κύριος Ἰησοῦς, ἡ θεία λειτουργία.
  800 + 888 + 8 + 25 + 929   = 2650.

Ἄνω τὰς καρδίας, Sursum corda, has the number 1688
or Κύριος Ἰησοῦς.

"Bring them hither to me" said the Lord.
Φέρετε μοι αὐτοὺς ὧδε.
915 + 120 + 1371 + 809   = 3215.

The same interpretation carries on.
Ἡ θεῖα λειτουργία, τὸ σημεῖον δυνάμεως.
8 + 25   + 929   + 370 + 383 + 1500   = 3215.
Ἰησοῦς τὸ δεῖπνον · Ἄνω   τὰς καρδίας.
888 + 370 + 269   + 851 + 501 + 336   = 3215.
Ἡ θεῖα λειτουργία, Λόγος Ὑιοῦ Κυρίου.   = 3215.

So the disciples were told to "make the men sit down."
This from St. John.
Ποιήσατε τοὺς ἀνθρώπους ἀναπέσειν.
674   + 970   + 1710   + 402   = 3756,
which will read,

Μυστήριον Ἰησοῦ Ὑιοῦ Κυρίου.
1178   + 688 + 880 + 1000   = 3756.

Σημεῖον, εὐχαριστία, ἐξουσία Κυρίου.
383   + 1627   + 746   + 1000   = 3756.

St. Luke's account gives here "make them sit down
by fifties in a company."
Κατακλίνατε αὐτοὺς κλισίας ὡσεὶ ἀνὰ πεντήκοντα.
738   + 1371 + 471 + 1015 + 52 + 884 = 4531.

Again the same idea
Μυστήριον Χριστὸς συγκοινωνός.
1178   + 1480   + 1873   = 4531.
Χριστὸς Κύριος ἡ μυστίκη σοφία Θεοῦ.
1480   + 800   + 1767   + 484   = 4531.
Φῶς ἀληθείας Κυρίου, ἡ μυστίκη σοφία.   = 4531.

The final word comes from St. John. "Gather up the
fragments that remain that nothing be lost."

Συναγάγετε τὰ περισσεύσαντα κλάσματα ἵνα μή
968 +301 +1552 +593 +61+48
τι ἀπόληται.
+310 +500 =4333,

which will again reproduce the mystery,

Κύριος ἐκκλησίας· Λόγος Κυρίου ἐνσώματος.

Lord of the Church : the Word of the Lord Incarnate,
(which is well typified in the preservation of every
fragment.)

Ἄνω τὰς καρδίας· Χριστὸς ἄρτος ἐκκλησίας. =4333.
Ἄρτος δυνάμεως Θεοῦ Σωτῆρος. =4333.

It may here be noted that

Εὐχαριστία+ὁ ἄρτος=2368='Ιησοῦς Χριστὸς,

and

Εὐχαριστία Κυρίου=2627=ὁ ἄρτος ἐκ τοῦ οὐρανοῦ.

There is certainly more to be discovered concerning
this feeding of the multitudes twice repeated, five loaves
and two fishes among five thousand and seven loaves
and a few fishes among four thousand, followed by
a special reminder of both miracles when the disciples
had forgotten to provision the boat. The number and
kind of the baskets used to collect the fragments is also
carefully noted in each case. And though St. Luke and
St. John omit the second miracle they keep strictly to
the twelve κόφινοι of the first. And readers may be
here reminded that this work is only a collection of
materials for study, and may be compared to the first
load of natural history specimens brought home by an
explorer. There is no "German thoroughness" about it.
Indeed its main use is to show that where these came
from there must needs be more to discover, and to
encourage other explorers.

WALKING ON THE SEA.

The next miracle will be the words spoken by the
Lord as He walked on the sea. St. Mark vi, 50.

"Be of good cheer. It is I. Be not afraid."
Θαρσεῖτε ἐγώ εἰμί.

$$630 + 808 + 65 = 1503$$

μὴ φοβεῖσθε.

$$48 + 801 = 849$$

$$= 2352.$$

The inner teaching, by gematria, would show that Love is the authority which casts out fear, since:—

Πλήρωμα ἀγάπης Κυρίου.

$$1059 + 293 + 1000 = 2352.$$

(Fulness of the Lord's Love).

The word divides into two sentences both in grammar and gematria.

The first is 1503

Θεὸς ὁ Λόγος ἐκ πατρὸς or Θεὸς Ἰχθύς.

The next is 849 which is ἡ μονὰς ἐν τριάδι or ἡ τριὰς ἐν μονάδι or ὁ τέλειος ἀνὴρ, etc.

The total is μυστήριον Λόγος ΑΩ.   = 2352.

τὸ πλοῖον μυστήριον ἐκκλησίας.   = 2352.

Here seems a very striking identification of the Lord with the Church.

The mystery which is the Word First and Last, is also the mystery which is the ship of the Church. Here the parables of the boat may be remembered (see p. 37).

THE GREEK WOMAN.

In the miracle wrought on the daughter of the Syrophenician woman, the two accounts in St. Matthew xv, 21 and St. Mark vii, 24 are so materially identical and so verbally divergent as to afford "a striking instance of the independence of the two narrations" (Alford). The outlook for satisfactory interpretation is not promising, especially as St. Matthew admits that the disciples were anxious to get rid of the woman. Our Lord moreover was outside the geographical limits of His Ministry. But it is noteworthy that while St. Matthew, a Hebrew, calls the woman a Canaanite, St. Mark emphasises the Greek element in his description of her.

Anyhow in St. Mark the word of power is :—

"For this saying go thy way."

διὰ	15
τουτὸν	1190
τὸν	420
λόγον	223
ὕπαγε	489
	2337

This gives

Χριστὸς Λόγος Θεοῦ · Christ, Word of God.

$$1480 + 373 + 484 = 2337.$$

The second part of the sentence, is ἐξελήλυθε τὸ δαιμόνιον ἐκ τῆς θυγατρός σου, 3513. We should analyse the gematria as follows :—

3513 = Ἑλληνὶς φῶς Χριστοῦ.

1145 + 2368 = Λόγος τῆς ἀληθείας Ἰησοῦ Χριστοῦ.

701 + 2812 = Ὑιὸς Δαβίδ · Φωνὴ τῆς ἐξουσίας.

2442 + 1071 = Καλὴ δύναμις Σωτῆρος · Σημεῖον Ἰησοῦ.

Ἡ Γνῶσις ἐκ Πνεύματος · Σημεῖον Ἰησοῦ.

1219 + 2294 = Ὁ Λόγος ἐκ Πατρός · Ἡ ζῶσα δύναμις Λόγου.

Ἰησοῦς ἐν σώματι.

Ὑιὸς Θεοῦ ὁμοούσιος.

Πλήρωμα Θεοῦ Πατρός.

With the ν added to ἐξελήλυθε(ν) 3513 becomes 3563, with the gematria

Κοινωνία ἁγίων Κυρίου Ἰησοῦ   = 3563.

The total of our Lord's words 2337 + 3513 is 5850, which may be interpreted as :—

5850 = Ἡ Γνῶσις τῶν μυστηρίων τοῦ Πατρός.

Ἰησοῦς Χριστός.   Δύναμις τῆς ἀληθείας τοῦ Θεοῦ Πατρός.
Ἡ μεγάλη φανέρωσις τοῦ Πατρός.
Χριστὸς ἐν σώματι · Ὁ Λόγος τοῦ Κυρίου Πατρός.
Χριστὸς ὁ Ὑιὸς Μεσσίας · Ὁ Λόγος τοῦ Κυρίου Πατρός.

A DEAF MAN.

In this miracle, St. Mark vii, 31, and in the next there seems great difficulty and strain on our Lord. A deaf person has to be reached. In this case, as in the next, he is brought and does not come, and it looks as if all the faith were in those who brought him, not in himself.

In the word Ephphatha, which is not Greek, there seems no gematria. But somewhere (we cannot verify the reference) the statement has been made that Ἐφφαθὰ Ἰησοῦς was a word of power. This would have the number 1904 which is that of Μονογένης Σωτήρ. But the Greek, διανοίχθητι = 1072, which would be ἡ ἀλήθεια Κυρίου, which was the idea to be conveyed to the deaf man.

A BLIND MAN.

In St. Mark viii, 22 there is again a miracle, at Bethsaida, that seems to give our Lord more than the ordinary trouble. A blind man is brought, that is, he does not come of his own accord. He has apparently to be led outside the village, more than the usual word or touch is required, but the only word spoken is the very brief "Seest thou aught," a Revisers' reading, it may be observed. εἴ τι βλέπεις; = 657, which is the sum of 284 θεὸς, and 373 Λόγος. The first response shows only partial success. The second effort however succeeds, but for some reason, probably to keep his faith firm, the man is not allowed to return to the village. But we have detected no further gematria.

THE BOY.

The next miracle to be described is the casting out of the devil from the boy in the village below the Mount of Transfiguration, St. Mark ix, 25. There is some indication of gematria in the colloquy with the father of the child, but the Lord was face to face with a devil of peculiar obstinacy, which had defied the rest of the disciples in the absence of the Lord and of his three chosen ones. And the words He used are longer and more emphatic than was His wont in such cases. This results in a very large number, correspondingly difficult to deal with.

It will be seen however that it is the exact double of a word already given. 4460 was the number of the question. "Who touched my clothes?" This number can be analysed as 2960 Ὑιὸς τοῦ ἀνθρώπου, and 1500 φῶς.

The text is, in the Revisers' Reading.

τὸ	370
πνεῦμα	576
τὸ	370
ἄλαλον	182
καὶ	31
κωφόν,	1440
ἐγώ	808
σοι	280
ἐπιτάσσω	1596
ἔξελθε	114
ἐξ	65
αὐτοῦ	1171
καὶ	31
μηκέτι	383
εἰσέλθῃς	467
εἰς	215
αὐτόν.	821
	——
	8920.

The number 8436 a multiple of 37 (37 × 228) added to 484 Θεοῦ gives the total 8920, but it is best to say that no means of dealing with so large a number are yet available. But there is a great similarity to 892 which has been dealt with, and in cases like this, the terminal cypher does not alter the significance.

BLIND BARTIMÆUS.
St. Mark x, 46—52.

This account of St. Mark's is selected from the other two, St. Matthew and St. Luke, which differ verbally. St. Matthew saying also that there were two blind men. St. Mark's seems to be the most graphic account, and has the speeches in oratia recta, (in all cases Revisers' Reading.) The blind man hardly attracts any attention or sympathy with his first call. "Jesus, Thou Son of David, have mercy on me," but his next, apparently only a variant, is

Ὑιε	415
Δαβίδ	21
ἐλέησὸν	368
μὲ	45
	849

a striking number in the Gnosis.

On which the Lord stands still, and gives the order φωνήσατε αὐτὸν. 2685 "Call him." This number suggests the interpretation ἡ φωνὴ, λόγος ἐξουσίας. The voice, a word of power.

And the Lord follows with
"What wilt thou that I do unto thee?"

Τί	310
θέλεις	259
ποιήσω	1168
σοι	280
	2017

and on this number there are :—

$\Phi\tilde{\omega}s \cdot {}^{\prime}\mathrm{H}\ \dot{a}\phi\acute{\eta}.$ = 2017.

$\beta\acute{a}\pi\tau\iota\sigma\mu a\ \sigma\eta\mu\epsilon\hat{\iota}o\nu\ K\nu\rho\acute{\iota}o\nu.$ = 2017.

$\dot{\eta}\ \gamma\nu\hat{\omega}\sigma\iota s + \dot{\epsilon}\xi o\upsilon\sigma\acute{\iota}a.$ = 2017.

The idea of Baptism is enlightenment or Light.

And the answer is

"Master that I may receive my sight."

$\mathrm{Pa}\beta\beta o\nu\acute{\iota}$	235
$\H{\iota}\nu a$	61
$\dot{a}\nu a\beta\lambda\acute{\epsilon}\psi\omega$	1589
	1885

which seems to acknowledge more than mere sonship of David for it stands for $K\acute{\nu}\rho\iota o s\ \Theta\epsilon\grave{o}s\ \mathrm{A}\Omega.$ 1885.

Already (p. 39) the answer has been partly interpreted, but the total of

$\H{\nu}\pi a\gamma\grave{\epsilon}\cdot {}^{\prime}\mathrm{H}\ \pi\acute{\iota}\sigma\tau\iota s\ \sigma o\upsilon\ \sigma\acute{\epsilon}\sigma\omega\kappa\acute{\epsilon}\ \sigma\epsilon$ = 3402.

The key to the gematria is the personal faith which is the Saviour and it is shown thus :—

${}^{\prime}\mathrm{H}\ \pi\acute{\iota}\sigma\tau\iota s\ \sigma o\hat{\upsilon}$ (Thy faith) = 1478 = $\dot{o}\ \Sigma\omega\tau\grave{\eta}\rho,$
and the rest of the sentence builds another of our 37 series :—

$\H{\Upsilon}\pi a\gamma\epsilon \ldots \sigma\acute{\epsilon}\sigma\omega\kappa\acute{\epsilon}\ \sigma\epsilon = 1924 = {}^{\prime}\mathrm{H}\ o\dot{\upsilon}\sigma\acute{\iota}a\ \Theta\epsilon o\hat{\upsilon}\ \Pi a\tau\rho\acute{o}s.$

$= X\rho\iota\sigma\tau\grave{o}s\cdot\Sigma\grave{a}\rho\xi\ \kappa a\grave{\iota}\ {}^{\prime\prime}\mathrm{A}\iota\mu a.$

3402.

Note that 1924 is $M\nu\sigma\tau\acute{\eta}\rho\iota o\nu$ 1178 + $\mathrm{E}\xi o\upsilon\sigma\acute{\iota}a$ 746.

But if the final ν be added this number becomes 3452 which may be

$K\acute{\nu}\rho\iota o s\ \Theta\epsilon\grave{o}s\ {}^{\prime}\mathrm{I}\eta\sigma o\hat{\upsilon}s\ X\rho\iota\sigma\tau\grave{o}s$ = 3452.

This however must still be regarded as unsettled.

Anyhow Bartimæus followed Jesus in the way to Jerusalem, and doubtless in what was called at first "The Way."

THE FIG TREE.

St. Mark xi, 14; also St. Matthew xxi, 18.

This is the last miracle recorded by St. Mark, and indeed the last of all before the Crucifixion, with the exception of the healing of the ear of Malchus in

Gethsemane. There is one preliminary problem to be cleared up—the hunger of the Lord, mentioned by both evangelists. This seems strange in the immediate vicinity of the most friendly and hospitable house of Lazarus in Bethany, but St. Matthew explains it in a word, ηὐλίσθη. They camped on the Mount of Olives, probably to avoid search and arrest at that house. And it was not impossible that the day's supply of food had been stopped or intercepted. At any rate a fig tree in full leaf was seen by the way side.

Sir W. Ramsay has a note on this (Pauline and other Studies, p. 242). After saying that in some parts, especially near the Dead Sea, figs have been said to be ripe during most of the year, such a thing was impossible at Easter at the altitude of Jerusalem. He continues, "That incident is one of the most difficult in the New Testament; and nothing that has been written about it seems of any value: but I am not prepared to offer any opinion. I do not see the way open to any explanation of the difficulty, whether in the way of moral teaching, or of erroneous popular mythology affecting in this case the Gospels. The passage is to me utterly obscure."

So says Sir W. Ramsay, and it may seem to need an apology if the problem be re-opened. Yet a solution seems possible, and personal observation of the fig trees in England suggests it.

The figs that ripen do so in the late summer among the green leaves. But there are figs of later growth that do not ripen but remain small and undeveloped on the tree during the winter, till frost kills them and they fall. But in the protection of a green-house they will last until in the spring the new young figs appear, reaching some little size before the leaf-buds expand. In the case of this barren fig tree the express statement is made that there was nothing but leaves on it. That

meant that there was no crop visible, and therefore no
sign of fertility either in the past year or in the coming
season. Or, to interpret the parable, no results under
the Law and no promise under the Gospel. The fig
tree was Jerusalem and its system, which was to be
suddenly destroyed. The actual fig tree was found
next morning far more withered than it would have
been if cut down. That was what astonished the disciples. It was destroyed by no ordinary process. This
is a case in which the gematria both in St. Mark and
St. Matthew becomes exegetical. The words of St. Mark
are

"No man eat fruit from thee henceforward for
ever," v, 14.

Μηκέτι ἐκ σοῦ εἰς τὸν αἰῶνα μηδεὶς καρπὸν
383 +25 +670 +215+420 +862 +267 +321
φάγοι
+584   = 3747.

Jerusalem had been the city of the Saints of the Lord.

Ἡ Ἰερουσαλὴμ Κοινωνία ἁγίων Κυρίου.
8 +864   +1875   +1000   = 3747.

The Law is done away and the covenant of Grace
stands in its place: so we see:—

Εὐαγγέλιον Κυρίου	1577
Μετάθεσις τοῦ νόμου	2170
	3747.
Ἐνιαυτὸς Κυρίου	2036
Νόμος χάριτος	1711
	3747.
Ἀποκάλυψις Κυρίου	2512
Τέλος Νόμου	1235
	3747.

Now take the parallel words in St. Matthew.

"Let there be no fruit from thee henceforward for ever."

Μηκέτι ἐκ σοῦ καρπὸς γένηται εἰς τὸν αἰῶνα.
383 + 25 + 670 + 471 + 377 + 215 + 420 + 862

$$= 3423.$$

Henceforth, Christ is the Way.

Ὁ Χριστὸς· ἡ πρόσφατος ὁδὸς.
1550   + 1873 $= 3423.$

Χάρις· 'Αποκάλυψις Κυρίου.
911   + 1512   + 1000 $= 3423.$

And there seems a reference to the communion of saints or the mystery of a visible church.

Τὸ μυστήριον	1548
κοινωνία ἁγίων	1875
	3423.

The wonder of the disciples at what they had seen drew from the Lord a repetition of His promise of still greater powers which could be exercised if sufficient faith were present.

St. Mark xi, 20; St. Matthew xxi, 20.

"But if ye shall say to this mountain 'Be thou removed and be thou cast into the sea' it shall be done."

῎Αρθητι	428
καὶ	31
βλήθητι	367
εἰς	215
τὴν	358
θάλασσαν	492
	1891.

Now 1891 = Οὐρανὸς Κυρίου.
> The Lord's Heaven.

> Οὐράνια βασιλεία Κυρίου.
> The Lord's Heavenly Kingdom.

> Ἡ κληρονομία Θεοῦ Κυρίου.
> The Inheritance of the Lord God.

and for Ὁ λόγος Κυρίου ὁ ἀληθινός.
> The True Word of the Lord.

> Ἡ μεγάλη δύναμις οὐρανοῦ.
> The Great Power of Heaven.

It will have been noted that 891, 892, 8920, etc., are gematria of "words of power" and it would appear that some transcendental energy is expressed by these numbers.

MIRACLES IN St. MATTHEW ONLY.

THE CENTURION.
TWO BLIND MEN.

THE CENTURION'S SERVANT.
St. Matthew viii, 13.

On the entry of the Lord in Capernaum, where the Lord's power to heal had been already displayed in the healing of the son of the Βασιλικὸς (probably Chuza, Herod's steward) by a message from afar, a centurion asks a similar favour for a sick slave, lying in helpless pain from paralysis. The Lord replies "I will come and heal him."

> Ἐγὼ ἐλθὼν θεραπεύσω αὐτόν.
> 808 + 894 + 1600 + 821 = 4123.

This will be some arrangement, it matters little which, of the words

> Ὁ Λόγος Θεοῦ, ἐξουσία τοῦ Χριστοῦ = 4123.
> "The Word of God: Authority of Christ."

The centurion knew that the word would do it. He knew also what ἐξουσία meant in his calling. And the Lord after comparing the soldier's marvellous faith with the slacker sort He had found in Israel uttered the word of power, "Go thy way, [and] as thou hast believed, so be it done unto thee."

The Revisers omit the "and", but in this case the gematria gives reason for retaining it. Of course its presence or absence makes no sort of difference to the plain meaning of the text.

The Greek then is:

Ὕπαγε, καὶ ὡς ἐπίστευσας γενηθήτω σοι.

489 + 31 + 1000 + 1401 + 1183 + 280 = 4384.

Now in both other cases where the Lord healed men sick of the palsy there is a decided reference to the power of the Lord to forgive sins. Of course, in the view of those who stood by, a centurion's slave would be a sinner of the Gentiles and his disease might be regarded as a punishment for his sins. And this is what is found in the number 4384

Σωτήρ, ἐξουσία Κυρίου ἀφιέναι ἁμαρτίας.

1408 + 746 + 1000 + 577 + 653 = 4384.

Λόγος κατὰ μυστήριον · μεγάλη ἐξουσία Σωτῆρος = 4384.

Still, if the καὶ be omitted, the number becomes 4353 on which are

Χριστὸς, Λόγος Κυρίου κατὰ μυστήριον,

or

Ψῆφος Κυρίου, κοινωνία ἁγίων.

The Lord intended to number such as this centurion into His kingdom.

THE TWO BLIND MEN.
St. Matthew ix, 29.

Here two blind men cry after the Lord as Son of David and follow Him until He and they enter the house, for it seems in this case, that it was important that no man should know it.

He asks them: "Believe ye that I am able to do this?"
Πιστεύετε ὅτι δύναμαι τοῦτο ποιῆσαι;
$1305 + 380 + 506 + 1140 + 379 = 3710$.

This may stand for ὁ ἐρχόμενος · φῶς Κυρίου $= 3710$.
Τὸ μυστήριον Θεοῦ Σωτῆρος. $= 3710$.
Χριστὸς ἐξουσία Θεοῦ Κυρίου. $= 3710$.

And their faith being proved by their reply, the Word
follows: "According to your faith be it unto you."

Κατὰ τὴν πίστιν ὑμῶν γενηθήτω ὑμῖν.
$322 + 358 + 650 + 1290 + 1183 + 500 = 4303$.

This may stand for:
Τὸ φῶς, Τὸ σημεῖον Χριστοῦ. $= 4303$.
Ἡ γνῶσις, τὸ μυστήριον Θεοῦ Κυρίου $= 4303$
and for a geometrical combination which we venture to
add
Μυστήριον Πεντέρημα, ζῶσα γεωμετρία ἀληθείας.
$1178 + 589 + 1008 + 1264 + 264 = 4303$.

For these expressions see our "Preliminary Investigation." $1178 + 589 = 1767$, on which are the following
phrases:

ἡ μυστικὴ σοφία $= 1767$.
ἡ Θεοῦ σοφία ἐκκλησίας $= 1767$.
κεκρυμμένον Πένταλφα $= 1767$.

MIRACLES IN ST. LUKE ONLY.

PASSING THE CROWD (see later).
THE DRAUGHT OF FISHES.
THE WIDOW'S SON.
THE CROOKED WOMAN.
THE DROPSY (no word spoken).
THE LEPERS.
MALCHUS.

THE DRAUGHT OF FISHES.
St. Luke v.

The miracle that immediately followed the conclusion of the parables recorded in St. Matthew xiii as preached from St. Peter's boat, is mentioned by St. Luke alone. When the Lord had finished speaking He said to Simon, "Launch out into the deep and let down your nets for a draught." We have already noted in Part I, p. 112 that

τὸ πλοῖον Σωτῆρος,

φωνὴ Κυρίου,

and

Πᾶς γραμματεὺς μαθητευθεὶς,

have each the number 2358.

This command is :—

Ἐπανάγαγε εἰς   τὸ βάθος καὶ χαλάσατε τὰ δίκτυα
149 +215+370+282+31   +1138+301 +735
ὑμῶν εἰς ἄγραν.
+1290+215+155=4881,

and this number gives us the number 2358 again with the addition of 2523.

Τὸ σημεῖον τοῦ Κυρίου,

370+383+770+1000=2523.

Ὁ Λόγος+τὸ ἅγιον πνεῦμα Κυρίου=2523,

and again 4881 gives us :—

Ὁ Λόγος, ὁ Σωτὴρ, Υἱὸς τοῦ ἀνθρώπου=4881.

After the night of unsuccessful fishing and the day's work of putting the nets in order, St. Peter is ready to obey the Lord's word with the result that it was all both boats could do to get the huge haul out of the overstrained nets into the overloaded boats. The exhibition of power frightened St. Peter, but the Lord's reply gave him courage anew and reminded him of an earlier promise, "Fear not, from henceforth thou shall catch men."

Μὴ φοβοῦ· ἀπὸ τοῦ νῦν ἀνθρώπους ἔσῃ ζωγρῶν.

48 + 1042 + 151 + 770 + 500 + 1710 + 213 + 1760

= 6194.

This number though large is readily analysed.

ἐξουσία Κυρίου (κόκκος σινάπεως)	= 1746.
Ἰησοῦς Χριστὸς (or Ἰησοῦ Χριστοῦ)	= 2368.
τὸ πνεῦμα ἅγιον Κυρίου	= 2080.
	6194.

It also gives

Ἁλιεῖς ἀνθρώπων (37 × 58)	= 2146.
(Fishers of men, St. Matthew iv, 18.)	
Τὸ μυστήριον (the Mystery)	= 1548.
Δυνάμεως Κυρίου (of the Power of the Lord)	= 2500.
	6194.

THE WIDOW'S SON.

In St. Luke vii, 11, is the story of the widow's son raised to life on the way to the tomb. No other evangelist tells of it and there is nothing said except the word of comfort to the mother "Weep not," μὴ κλαῖε, with the number 114, which is too small to be significant by itself, and the word that bade the dead arise. This is "Young man, I say unto thee, arise."

Νεανίσκε, σοὶ λέγω ἐγέρθητι.

341 + 280 + 838 + 440 = 1899

and neither on this nor on the sum of the numbers 114 + 1899 = 2013 can any gematria be found.

The natural conclusion would be that there is none intended. But by venturing to substitute the articular nominative for the vocative so good a result appears, both here and in the case of Lazarus, that the experiment is justifiable. By substituting 676, ὁ νεανίσκος for 341 we get 2234 which gives

Χριστὸς ἡ ἐξουσία = 2234

and with 114 added 2348 which gives

Τὸ μυστήριον κεκρυμμένον, 2348.

See notes on Jairus' daughter and Lazarus.

THE CROOKED WOMAN.

In St. Luke xiii, 10, we have the miracle of the healing of the bent woman, where the infirmity is directly attributed to Satan. Satan had bound her, ἔδησεν, and she was loosed from this bond, δεσμός. The words are "Woman thou art loosed from thine infirmity:"

Γύναι, ἀπολέλυσαι ἀπὸ τῆς ἀσθενείας σοῦ. = 3101

on this number we have:—

Ἰησὸῦς ὁ λόγος τοῦ Κυρίου = 3101.

Ἡ δεσμία Σατανᾶ+Χριστὸς Κύριος = 3101

where the captive of Satan meets with Christ the Lord.

There are some other combinations with the number 800 such as:

Σατανᾶς τὸ μυστήριον κόσμου = 3101.

But the power of Christ is also in evidence.

Ἰησοῦς ἡ δύναμις κατὰ μυστήριον = 3101.

But here again if the articular nominative is used ἡ γύνη, the number becomes 3106.

Ἰησοῦς · ἀφέσις ἁμαρτίων.

Ἰησοῦς ὁ σωτήρ ἐκ παρθένου.

Σημεῖον Ἰησοῦ · σοφία τοῦ Θεοῦ.

Γνῶσις τῆς ἀληθειας.

Φωνὴ μετανοίας.

Ἰλασμὸς Θεοῦ Κυρίου.

Ὁ λόγος Κυρίου · ὁ προφορικὸς λόγος.

Ὁ λόγος Θεοῦ · ὁ Σωτήρ, υἱὸς Δάβιδ.

Ἐξουσία · φωνή τῆς ἐκκλησίας (or) ὁμολογίας.

Ὁ Λόγος τῆς μετανοίας · ὁ Σωτήρ.

One asks: What is the true relation of Satan to sickness?

THE TEN LEPERS.
St. Luke xvii, 11.

In this miracle ten men that were lepers stand afar off, for they were cut off from the congregation, and cry for mercy. One was a Samaritan. The answer of the Lord is:—Go show yourselves to the priests.

Πορευθέντες ἐπιδείξατε ἑαυτοὺς τοῖς ἱερεῦσι (ν).

1224   +480   +1376+580   +730

                             =4390 or 4440.

The gematria seems connected with the Church, which-
ever of the two numbers is taken. Samaritan and all,
they were to be restored.

ἐκκλησία · τὸ θυσιαστήριον Ἰησοῦ Χριστοῦ.

294   +1728   +2368   =4390.

This number may also be :

ἐξουσία Κυρίου · Χριστὸς Ὑιὸς Θεοῦ.   =4390.

The alternative, adding the ν, is 37×120   =4440.

Ἡ ἐκκλησία τοῦ Κυρίου Ἰησοῦ Χριστοῦ   =4440.

The Church of the Lord Jesus Christ,
or as a title of the Lord

Χριστὸς, Ὑιὸς τοῦ ἀνθρώπου   =4440.

Christ, (the) Son of Man.

MALCHUS.

The last miracle recorded by St. Luke xxii, 51, in
fact the last miracle of our Lord's ministry before His
Passion—His last free act, is the healing of the High
Priest's Servant, whose name, Malchus, St. John gives.
This victim of St. Peter's clumsy swordmanship had his
ear cut off, though it seems to have hung still on the
man's cheek. The Lord asked leave, touched it, and
healed it. The words are

" Suffer me thus far "

Ἐᾶτε ἕως τούτου= 2856.

On this number we have

Μυστήριον σωτῆρος, 2856

and also the locality where the miracle was done

Τὸ ὅρος τῶν ἐλαιῶν   =2856.

The Mount of Olives,
also those phrases already given

Ὁ Χριστὸς, μεθ' ἡμῶν ὁ θεός

Ἰησοῦς, ὁ Ἐμμανουὴλ τοῦ Θεοῦ.

Θεὸς σωτὴρ Ὑιὸς Θεοῦ.

It was the last manifestation of the power hitherto so freely exercised. From that moment onwards to the rending of the veil it was His enemies' hour and "The Power of Darkness" Ἡ ἐξουσία τοῦ σκοτοῦς = 2784 = Φῶς Θεοῦ κεκρυμμένον. The Light of God hidden.

MIRACLES IN St. JOHN ONLY.

THE WINE AT CANA.
THE NOBLEMAN'S SON.
THE POOL OF BETHESDA.
THE POOL OF SILOAM.
LAZARUS.

The second chapter of St. John contains the record of what was actually the first of our Lord's miracles, though it was not recognised as such by all who saw it. His blessed Mother's faith urged it on Him, and evidence will be submitted that it was she who sent for Him for the second miracle also. We cannot be certain of any gematria in her first words Ὄινον οὐκ ἔχουσι, where the problem of the final ν, not yet solved, also suggests caution.

But His first words "Woman, what have I to do with thee, mine hour is not yet come" divide into two clauses, each of which, and the whole, are significant.

Τί	310
ἐμοὶ	125
καὶ	31
σοί	280
γύναι ;	464
	1210

A number which gives
Ὁ Μεσσίας Θεοῦ. 70+656+484 = 1210.
Ὁ ἐρχόμενος. = 1210.

He is more than Ὁ οἰνόχοος, 1210, the wine-pourer
and there seems some holy mystery which suggests
that He may be the bearer of the Grail with the wine
of the Spirit that is to come

παράκλητος + οἶνος = 1210.

Also has the Blessed Virgin authority?
Ἡ Μήτηρ + ἐξουσία = 464 + 746 = 1210.

There may also be some geometry, for 1210 is the
circumference of the circle whose diameter is ἡ ῥάβδος
the Rod (of the stem of Jesse).

Τὸ πνεῦμα ἀλήθειας⎫ = 1210.
ἀλήθεια πνευμάτος ⎭

The second part of the words is

οὔπω	1350
ἥκει	43
ἡ	8
ὥρα	901
μου	510
	2812 = 37 × 76.

His hour is not yet come, but He is

Ἰησοῦς ἡ οὐσία Θεοῦ πατρός.   = 2812.

Jesus the substance of God the Father,
or any of the following, indicating the Trinity, come on
the same number.

Ὑιὸς τοῦ παντοκράτορος
Ὁ Ὢν, ὁ Παντοκράτωρ
Τὸ πνεῦμα ἅγιον. ἡ ἄρχη ζωῆς.

The total of these 1210 + 2812 is 4022 and on this
number may be found :

Ὁ Μεσσίας, ὁ Χριστὸς, ἐξουσία Κυρίου,
Χριστὸς, ὁ Σωτὴρ, ἀληθεία Κυρίου,
and perhaps others.

The response of the Blessed Mother is to the servants.
Whatsoever He saith unto you, do it.

Ὅ	70
τι	310
ἂν	51
λέγῃ	46
ὑμῖν	500
ποιήσατε	674
	1651.

Α. Ω. Ἀμὴν πατρὸς.
Δυνάμις ἐξουσίας.

Which gives a wondrous law.

νόμος θαυμαστὸς	1651.
θεότης πλήρωμα	1651.
Κύριος + ὕπαρξις.	1651.

Now come the words of power. The six great water-pots stand near, ready to contain water in quantities calculated for washing rather than drinking. "Fill the water-pots with water."

γεμίσατε	564
τὰς	501
ὑδρίας	715
ὕδατος	975
	2755 ἡ γνῶσις Θεοῦ Κυρίου

This will equal

Ἰησοῦς σημεῖον	1271	or ἡ γνῶσις
Θεοῦ	484	
Κυρίου	1000	
	2755.	

The servants obeyed with a will; and if it be lawful to add to the above number 2755

       ἕως ἄνω 1856   to the brim.

          4611

The result will give

Κύριος Ἰησοῦς Χριστὸς ὁ Λόγος Κυρίου.

Τὸ σημεῖον Κυρίου · φωνὴ δυνάμεως.

Anyhow if these extra words were not in the order they were obeyed in its execution.

Then came the next command: " Draw out now and bear to the governor of the feast."

Ἀντλήσατε	895
νῦν	500
καὶ	31
φέρετε	915
τῷ	1100
ἀρχιτρικλίνῳ	2031
	5472

a large number which admits of this

φωνὴ Κυρίου	2358
ἐξουσία	746
Ἰησοῦ Χριστοῦ	2368
	5472

and probably far more could be found. These words may also be transposed thus

Ἐξουσία Κυρίου (Κόκκος σινάπεως) φωνὴ Ἰησοῦ Χριστοῦ.

Τὸ μυστήριον Ἰησοῦ · ἐκπόρευσις πνεύματος Κυρίου.

The words of the ruler of the feast seem worthy of study. He spoke all unconsciously a truth as well as a compliment to the bridegroom.

Σὺ	600
τετήρηκας	942
τὸν	420
καλὸν	171
οἶνον	250
ἕως	1005
ἄρτι	411
	3799

which seems to be:

$$\begin{array}{ll} \text{'Εξουσία Κυρίου,} & 1746 \\ \text{Λόγος Χριστοῦ } 373+1680, & 2053 \\ \hline & 3799. \end{array}$$

These words may be an example of a "Tongue." At any rate the Evangelist thinks it deserving of a place.

THE NOBLEMAN'S SON.

The second miracle that Jesus did when He was come out of Judæa into Galilee has a notable word attached to it, with a possible exegetical value of an interesting personal sort, helping, maybe to identify the people spoken of. Our Lord was at Cana again on this occasion when a certain Βασιλικὸς, or man about the court of Herod, heard that Jesus was come out of Judæa and went to call Him to heal his son who was ill of fever, and returned with the answer, "Go thy way, thy son liveth," believing that it would be so.

$$\begin{array}{ll} \text{Πορεύου} & 1125 \\ \text{ὁ} & 70 \\ \text{υἱός} & 680 \\ \text{σοῦ} & 670 \\ \text{ζῇ} & 15 \\ \hline & 2560 \end{array}$$

At the first trial this number resolved itselt into
2368 Ἰησοῦς Χριστός and
192 Μαριάμ
———
2560.

Now in chapter ii, 12 we are distinctly told that our Lord and His mother and His brethren came to live at Capernaum, and it may well be that His Mother was there at this time. Can the Blessed Virgin have had a share in this miracle also? Who can the Βασιλικός have been? Try Chuza, Herod's steward, whose wife was Joanna. See!

The Miracles.

Μαριὰμ	192
μητὴρ	456
Κυρίου	1000
	1648
Ἰωάννα	912
	2560.

2560. There is the number!

One more interpretation shows itself.

Μυστήριον	1178
ἐκκλησίας	494
	1672
with 888	Ἰησοῦς

2560 The same again!

And was not Joanna probably at the Cross and certainly at the Tomb. Did she not minister of her substance? Was not this the reason or one reason?

THE POOL OF BETHESDA.

The miracle of the healing of the impotent man at the Pool of Bethesda has a point in common with the healing of the sick of the palsy in that it is connected with the power to forgive sins. The man when met in the temple is told to sin no more lest a worse thing happen to him. He therefore had some sin to be forgiven. The first word of the Lord is "Wilt thou be made whole?"

Θέλεις	259
ὑγιὴς	621
γένεσθαι	383
	1163.

The word of Emmanuel asks this.

Τὸ	370
Ῥῆμα	149
Ἐμμανουήλ	644
	1163.

Then comes the word of power: "Arise, take up thy bed, and walk." For the pool, and whatever mystery connected with it, had proved of no use in this case, as the man, though believing in it, explains.

Ἔγειραι ·	134
ἆρον	221
τὸν	420
κράββατόν	546
σοῦ	670
καὶ	31
περιπάτει	591
	2613.

This gives the sign of the Lord to forgive sins.

Σημεῖον	383	
Κυρίου	1000	Θεότης · πλήρωμα θεοτήτος.
ἀφιέναι	577	ὁ Μεσσίας · σωτήριον Ἰσραὴλ.
ἁμαρτίας	653	ἐκκλησία σωτήρ · εὔκαιρος βοήθεια.
	2613	

The words common to this miracle and to the healing of the sick of the palsy are Ἔγειραι ἆρον τὸν κράββατόν σου, counting 1991. This is the sum of ὁ Λόγος and τὸ μυστήριον.

But if the whole of the Lord's words be added together, 1163 + 2613 the sum is 3776, a very remarkable total.

First comes

Ἐξουσία Κυρίου (κόκκος σινάπεως)	1746
ἀφιέναι ἁμαρτίας	1230
κόσμου.	800
	3776.

Power of the Lord to forgive the sins of the world. Thus

Ἰησοῦς Χριστὸς Σωτὴρ   2368 + 1408 = 3776.

This is the sum of 888 Ἰησοῦς and 2888 the Kingdom of Heaven, ἡ Βασιλεία τῶν οὐρανῶν, which has a geometrical connection with Melchisedec. Ὁ λόγος Θεοῦ· μόνος Κύριος σωτηρίας = 3776.

But to conclude. One part of our Lord's final words to this man is identical with what He said to the woman taken in adultery. "From henceforth sin no more." And this has grave significance.

Ἀπὸ τοῦ   νῦν μηκέτι ἁμάρτανε.
151 + 770 + 500 + 383   + 498   = 2302.

It stands for this

Τὸ ῥῆμα Ἐμμανουήλ   1163   as above.
κρατεῖν, to retain,   486
ἁμαρτίας, sins,   653
―――――
2302.

THE MAN BORN BLIND.

In this chapter the disciples call the Lord's attention to a case of suffering which according to a theory that they seemed to hold, and which is still held by many in the world of to-day, that such suffering must be merited. The Lord does not deal with that question at all, but anoints the man's eyes with clay made with His spittle and says "Go to the Pool of Siloam and wash."

Ὕπαγε νίψαι εἰς τὴν κολυμβήθραν τοῦ Σιλωάμ,
489 + 771 + 215 + 358   + 730   + 770   + 1081
= 4414.

Τὸ ὕδωρ· ἡ παρουσία φωτός.   The Water : The Advent of Light.   = 4414.

Ἡ ἐξουσία τῆς γεωμετρίας Κυρίου Ἰησοῦ.   = 4414.

Λόγος Κυρίου· ἡ δύναμις τῆς καθάρσεως Θεοῦ   = 4414.

Χριστὸς ὁ Μεσσίας· Σωτὴρ κόσμου.   = 4414.

The number is very definitely one of the mystical geometry, consisting as it does, of 2178+2236. The first of these is the μυστήριον Κυρίου, so often alluded to in our researches, and the second stands for the root of the number five.   4414 is alternatively 2000+2414, the proportionals of the Octagon, the symbol of regeneration by the cleansing power of Baptism.   So we find that by this gematria, Christ, the Messiah is also

'Ο Κύριος τοῦ βαπτίσματος τοῦ κόσμου.
The Lord of the Baptism of the world　　=4414.

It is also worthy of note that the waters of Siloam, Τὰ ὕδατα τοῦ Σιλωὰμ 2858 = Μυστήριον Χριστοῦ, or Θησαυρὸς φωτός, and that 2858 = 2178+680, thus reading Μυστήριον Κυρίου, plus the word κολυμβήθρα or Pool which, like τὸ πλοῖον, the Lord's Boat, has the number of the Son, 680.

The passage is further complicated by the interpretation "sent" (ἀπέσταλμένος).   The number of this word in 982 in which we trace some remarkable combinations, which may throw light on the doubtful point as to who or what is meant.   Was it Christ who was "sent"?   The man?   The pool?

Ἰησοῦς	888
Ἀπεσταλμένος	982

　　　　1870 = Τὸ φῶς.　The Light (symbol of Baptism).

or

Ὑιὸς	680
Ἀπεσταλμένος	932

　　　　1662 = Μυστήριον Θεοῦ or Ἐπιφανεία Κυρίου.

Then follows a long argumentative discussion with neighbours and Pharisees.   Briefly, it was a case of theory versus fact.   Some one once spoke of the tragedy that was enacted when a beautiful theory was murdered by a fact.

The Pharisees cast the man out of the synagogue. Facts that contradict authority are regarded as most noxious things.

But the Lord met the poor excommunicate and spoke to him saying,

"Dost thou believe in the Son of God?"

Σὺ πιστεύεις εἰς τὸν υἱὸν τοῦ Θεοῦ;
600 + 1210 + 215 + 420 + 530 + 770 + 484 = 4229.

There had been a "sending," perhaps of two sorts. A sending of the Son, and the sending to the pool.

Ὑιὸς Κύριος ἀπεσταλμένος, ἡ ἀποστολὴ Κυρίου.
680 + 800 + 982 + 8 + 759 + 1000

2462 1767 = 4229.

Ὑιὸς Κύριος = 1480 = Χριστός.

2462 = Μυστήριον κεκρυμμένον Θεοῦ.

And 1767 is the number of the Μυστήριον πεντέρημα of the Pistis Sophia restoration.

1549 + 2680 = 4229 = Τὸ Ἀ΄ μυστήριον Χριστοῦ Κυρίου.
4229 Ἡ γνῶσις τοῦ Ἰησοῦ κατὰ μυστήριον.

The man wants to know in whom he is to believe and the answer is: "Thou hast both seen Him and it is He that talketh with thee."

Καὶ ἑώρακας αὐτὸν καὶ ὁ λάλων μετὰ σοῦ ἐκεῖνός
31 + 1127 + 821 + 31 + 70 + 911 + 346 + 670 + 360
ἐστιν.
+ 565 = 4932.

This is a large number on which the following can be found.

Ἰησοῦς Χριστός, τὸ ἅγιον πνεῦμα Θεοῦ Κυρίου = 4932.
Φῶς μυστήριον τοῦ Θεοῦ Κυρίου = 4932.

There may be others also.

But what our Lord insists on is the sin of being wilfully blind to facts.

LAZARUS.

The miracle of the raising of Lazarus has already been referred to incidentally but there is much in the whole story that will bear close attention.

Searching first the most likely parts, the answer of the Lord on receiving the sister's message is

"This sickness is not unto death"

Αὕτη ἡ ἀσθενεία οὐκ ἔστι (ν) πρὸς θάνατον.

709+8 +281+490+515(50)+450 +481 = 2934

for which we may read

Υἱὸς τοῦ Θεοῦ Κυρίου = 2934

or with the ν added = 2984.

"But for the glory of God."

Ἀλλ᾽ ὑπὲρ τῆς δόξης τοῦ Θεοῦ.

61 +585+508+342+770+484   = 2750.

"That the Son of God may be glorified thereby."

Ἵνα δοξασθῇ ὁ υἱὸς τοῦ Θεοῦ δι᾽ αὐτῆς.

61 +352+70+680+770+484+14+909   = 3340.

$$\overline{6090.}$$

The first of these numbers may be taken either as containing the ν or not. If it be 2934 the interpretation may be

Φῶς ἐξουσία Ἰησοῦ = 2934,

or

Υἱὸς τοῦ Θεοῦ Κυρίου = 2934.

If it be 2984 this idea still remains

Φῶς Θεοῦ Κυρίου = 2984.

The second number is 2750 which gives

Τὸ φῶς Υἱοῦ   = 2750

and the third is

Σταυρὸς ἀπαύγασμα δόξης Κυρίου

Ὁ Υἱὸς · ἀπαύγασμα δόξης τοῦ Πατρός   = 3340.

$$\overline{6090.}$$

These numbers must be coupled, and the total is 6090, which is

Χριστὸς ὁ λόγος τοῦ πατρὸς ἐκ τῶν οὐρανῶν.

1480 +443   +1521+25+1150+1471 = 6090

or

Ἰησοῦς Χριστὸς Κύριος ζώντων ἄνωθεν.

888 +1480 +800 +2007 +915   = 6090.

The discourse that follows, concerning the danger of a return to Judæa, leads up to the need for light and then to the quite explicit statement that Lazarus was dead. So they go to Bethany. But that statement contains the promise of resurrection.

Our friend Lazarus sleepeth.
Λάζαρος ὁ φίλος ἡμῶν κεκοίμηται.
409 + 70 + 810 + 898   + 484   = 2671.
'Αλλὰ πορεύομαι ἵνα ἐξυπνίσω αὐτόν.
62   + 776 + 61   + 1605 + 821   = 3325.

In these numbers we seem to find traces of a sign of resurrection given in another place by the Lord in the sign of the prophet Jonah. The word Jonah means "dove," the Greek for which is περιστερὰ, with the number 801, which is also ΑΩ.

And τὸ σημεῖον ΑΩ or τὸ σημεῖον περιστερά, enumerates at 1554 on which also comes

Μεσσίας ἡμῶν.
Ζωόγονος θεός.
'Ανάστασις σαρκός.

And 1554 added to 2358 (φωνὴ Κυρίου) gives Τὸ σημεῖον 'Ιωνᾶ τοῦ προφήτου. The sign of the prophet Jonah. And 2671 gives ὁ ὕπνος Κυρίου ΑΩ, from which there is a great awakening, and 3325 Κύριος ἡ ἀνάστασις 1771 to add to 1554 = 3325.

Such was the promise, repeated in other words when Bethany was reached.

"Thy brother shall rise again."
'Αναστήσεται ὁ ἀδελφός σου.
1076 + 70 + 810 + 670   = 2626
on which come :—
'Η 'Αλήθεια Κυρίου, ἀνάστασις σαρκός   = 2626.
'Εξουσία 'Υιοῦ Κυρίου   = 2626.

The resurrection of the dead was already a strong belief, but the Lord's reply was this : " I am the Resurrection and the Life."

> Ἐγὼ εἰμι ἡ ἀναστάσις καὶ ἡ ζώη.
> 808+65+8   +963 +31+8+815   = 2698

which by gematria yields the interpretation :—

> Ἰησοῦς ὁ Μεσσίας · ἡ Θεότης Θεοῦ.
> 888+70 +656 +8 +592+484   = 2698.
>
> Ἰησοῦς ὁ Μεσσίας · Θεὸς · Κύριος.
> Ἐμμανουὴλ τοῦ Θεοῦ · Κύριος.
> 644   +770+484 +800   = 2698.
>
> Ἰησοῦς · ἀληθινὸς Μεσσίας ἐκ Πατρός.
> 888   +378   +656+25   +751   = 2698,

and again

> "He that believeth on Me, though he were dead, yet shall he live."
>
> Ὁ πιστεύων εἰς ἐμὲ, κἂν ἀποθάνῃ, ζήσεται.
> 70 +1845+215+50+71 +219   +531 = 3001,

where the gematria emphatically shows who He is on Whom we must believe, to have life :—

> Χριστὸς τοῦ Πατρός.
> 1480+770 +751   = 3001.
>
> Ἰησοῦς · Θεότης τοῦ Πατρός.
> 888 +592+770 +751   = 3001.
>
> Ἰησοῦς Χριστὸς · Ἅγιὸς Ἰσραήλ.
> 888 +1480 +284 +349   = 3001.
>
> Ἰησοῦς ὁ ἐνεργὴς Λόγος · Ζὼη Θεοῦ.
> 888+70 +371 +373+815+484   = 3001.
>
> Λόγος Κυρίου · Ἀναγέννησις ἐκ νεκρῶν.
> 1373   +1628   = 3001.
>
> Ἰησοῦς ὁ Ὑιὸς Δαβίδ · Βασιλεὺς ἐκκλησίας.
> 888 +750   +21   +848   +494   = 3001,

and the combined gematria will be 2698+3001 = 5699, which readily resolves itself into the following :—

> Jesus the Saviour : the Word of the Lord God Incarnate.
>
> Ἰησοῦς ὁ Σὼτηρ · ὁ Λόγος Κυρίου Θεοῦ ἐν σώματι.
> 2366   +443   +1484   +1406 = 5699,

with an immensley rich field of parallel gematria, for
which we have no space.

The saying of Jesus concludes with the words

"And whosoever liveth and believeth on Me shall
never die."

Καὶ πᾶς ὁ ζῶν καὶ πιστεύων εἰς ἐμὲ οὐ μὴ ἀποθάνῃ
31   +1208 +31   +1845 +265 +518   +219
εἰς τὸν αἰῶνα
        +1497   = 5614,
but this is

Jesus Christ, Messiah : Godhead of Godhead : the
Resurrection.

Ἰησοῦς Χριστὸς · Μεσσίας · θεότης θεοτήτος · ἡ ἐξανά-
2368   +656   +592   +962   +1036
στασις.
                                = 5614.

Ἰησοῦς Χριστὸς · Λόγος Κυρίου · Λόγος κατὰ μυστήριον.
                                = 5614.

Ἰησοῦς Χριστὸς Λόγος Κυρίου · Μεσίτης · Τὰ πάντα
καὶ ἐν πᾶσι   = 5614,

and perhaps a hundred other equally good interpretations
based upon the recurring multiples of the "metacubic"
number 37, with the characteristic word "Messiah" or
"Mediator" included.

All this takes place while the Lord is still in the
place where Martha met Him. He has not entered the
village. Now begins the journey to the tomb.

"Where have ye laid him?"

Ποῦ τεθείκετε αὐτόν;
550   +659 +821   = 2030.

Ἡ ὁδὸς σωτῆρος   = 2030.

The way of the Saviour begins, and His next word
is spoken when the tomb is reached.

"Take ye away the stone,"

Ἄρατε τὸν λίθον.   = 996.

Ἡ ὁδὸς Ἐμμανουήλ.   = 996.

All the way there had been doubt and even unbelief. At last there was even protest. The order struck a natural horror, but was obeyed on a further appeal for faith.

> "Said I not unto thee that if thou wouldest believe thou shouldest see the glory of God."

Οὐκ εἶπόν σοι ὅτι ἐὰν πιστεύσῃς ὄψει τὴν δόξαν
490+215+280 +380+56   +1403 +785+358 +185
τοῦ Θεοῦ.
+770+484   = 5406.

This gives the following :

Ἰησοῦς, Χριστός Θεοῦ Κυρίου, ἀνάστασις σαρκός. = 5406.

Jesus the Christ of the Lord God, Resurrection of the flesh.

This may be taken as 4033 (= 37 × 109) with the addition of 1000+373 (Λόγος Κυρίου).

Λόγος Κυρίου · σωτὴρ κόσμου · ἡ ἀνάστασις καὶ ἡ ζωὴ
                                                        = 5406.

Or as 3811 (37 × 103) with the addition of 1595 = πίστεως, which makes it

Christ All and in all: the Power of Faith.

Τὰ πάντα καὶ ἐν πᾶσι Χριστὸς = 2590.

Η δύναμις τῆς πίστεως   = 2816.
                                  ⎯⎯⎯⎯
                                  5406.

Then follows the Lord's thanksgiving, spoken aloud for the sake of those that stood by. For it may well have been that what Martha had said was actually the case, and anyhow faith was still very weak.

'Father, I thank thee that thou hast heard me."

Πάτερ, εὐχαριστῶ σοι   ὅτι ἤκουσάς μου.
486   +2416 +280+380+899 +510   = 4971.

This may be taken as

The teaching of the Knowledge of the Lord.

Ἡ διδαχὴ τῆς γνώσεως τοῦ Κυρίου.   = 4971.

or

The Power of God.

'Η δύναμις Θεοῦ   = 1197.

Jesus Christ in the Body.

'Ιησοῦς Χριστὸς ἐν σώματι = 3774.

$$\overline{\quad\quad}$$
4971.

And the rest of the thanksgiving enumerates as follows, divided into its clauses.

"And I knew that thou hearest me always,"

'Εγὼ δὲ ᾔδειν ὅτι πάντοτέ μου ἀκούεις.

808 + 9 + 77 + 380 + 806 + 510 + 706   = 3296.

"But because of the multitude that stand by I said it,"

'Αλλὰ διὰ τὸν ὄχλον τὸν περιεστῶτα εἶπον.

62 + 15 + 420 + 820 + 420 + 1801 + 215 = 3753.

"That they may believe that thou didst send me."

Ἵνα πιστεύσωσιν ὅτι σύ με ἀπέστειλας.

61 + 2255 + 380 + 600 + 45 + 832 = 4173.

The first of these may read

Θεὸς 'Ιησοῦς Χριστὸς 'Εμμανουήλ. = 3296.

The second

Τὸ σημεῖον· ἐξουσία τοῦ Θεοῦ Κυρίου. = 3753.

The third

'Ο Κύριος 'Ισραὴλ · Σωτὴρ ἐκ τοῦ πατρός. = 4173.

Then came the climax. Forthwith the Lord, changing His voice to a loud cry, called "Lazarus come forth."

As the text stands this is

Λάζαρε δεῦρο ἔξω. = 1588.

On this number we find

The Word of the Spirit of Love.

Ρῆμα πνεύματος ἀγάπης.

149 + 1146 + 293 = 1588.

The Resurrection, God's covenant.

Η ἐξανάστασις· ἡ διαθήκη Θεοῦ = 1588.

But on the other hand we may substitute the peremptory articular nominative used in other cases where the spiritual world is addressed. The ordinary vocative which is in the text of the miracle at Nain gives no results, while the articular nominative does—if ὁ νεάνισκος may be read for νεάνισκε.

So it is here suggested that ὁ Λάζαρος δεῦρο ἔξω with the gematria of Χριστὸς ὁ Λόγος = 1923 is probably a proper reconstruction.

The final word spoken at the open and now empty tomb is "Loose him and let him go."

Λύσατε αὐτὸν, καὶ ἄφετε αὐτὸν ὑπάγειν.

936 + 821 + 31 + 811 + 821   + 549   = 3969.

On this number we find

2368 + 800 + 801 = Ἰησοῦς Χριστὸς Κύριος Α.Ω.

and

The "Christ, Lord of Salvation."

Ὁ Χριστὸς · Κύριος σωτηρίας.

1550   + 800   + 1619   = 3969,

and a phrase which combines the Incarnation with the Resurrection

Ἡ ἀνάστασις,   = 971.

Ὁ Χριστὸς Κυρίου ὁ ἀληθινὸς   = 2998.

————

3969

or ὁ Υἱὸς Κυρίου ἐκ τῆς Παρθένου, which is also 2998.

The second αὐτὸν is omitted by some MSS. but the text as given follows the Revisers' reading.

MIRACLES OF UNSEEN ESCAPE.

The above title we may apply to a group of Miracles remaining, which, from their very nature could have had no words of power attached to them, and in connection with which, nothing but the bare statement of the fact alleged appears to be available for our purpose.

No emphasis is laid upon the miraculous character of the phenomena described, yet there are present in these conditions quite inconsistent with physical laws of motion within the limits of the Space we know. The abnormal element is quietly assumed.

Three such cases are related in connection with our Lord. Once He escapes from a hostile crowd at Nazareth which desires to throw Him over a cliff. The other two cases occur in the Temple at Jerusalem.

Apart from these, there is also the instance of St. Philip the Deacon when the Spirit of the Lord caught him away; and that of the release of the Apostles and of St. Peter from prison may also be included, although in those cases the escape is attributed to an Angel. But, as with the charisms, so with the miracles, it is the self-same Spirit working in all, and through many agencies.

With the Miracles of "escape" may be classed such phenomena as our Lord's walking on the sea, and St. Peter's attempt to do so. For this there is a modern term "levitation," which is perhaps more or less applicable.

Now from the earliest days of our study of the gematria, especially in the case of that which is contained in the Coptic Gnostic books, it has been evident that that gematria, whether consciously or intuitively, is framed to describe in the mathematics of geometry the symmetric ratios governing cosmic form and order, and from these as a basis, stretching forth to the concept of a Greater Universe transcending the limitations of Space and Time, yet equally subject to Divine Law as expressible, not by material symbol, but in the transcendent language of mathematics.

Hence when dealing with such passages in the Scriptures as concern the higher verities, as do these miracles, we claim to be justified in applying to the

Greek text the same test that we have successfully
applied in the case of the Coptic Books which actually
deal with the teachings said to have been imparted by
Jesus to His disciples after His Resurrection. So we
proceed to examine the gematria of these passages.
Let us first take the words in St. Luke xiv, 30.
" But He, passing through the midst of them, went His
way." Αὐτὸς δὲ διελθὼν διὰ μεσοῦ αὐτῶν ἐπορεύετο.
The gematria is 5204, and we find these equivalents:—

5204 = Φῶς Μυστήριον · Ἡ γεωμετρία τοῦ Θεοῦ.
Ἡ γεωμετρία · Μυστήριον δυνάμεως τοῦ Θεοῦ.
Φῶς · Ἔνδυμα Ἰησοῦ · Ἐξουσία τοῦ Κυρίου.
Ἡ σωτηρία Θεοῦ · Ἡ Γνῶσις τοῦ μείζονος κόσμου.
Ὁ Υἱὸς τοῦ Θεοῦ · Μυστήριον τοῦ μείζονος κόσμου.
Γνῶσις τῆς ἀληθείας · ἡ δύναμις τῆς γεωμετρίας Θεοῦ
Μέγας παραλήμπτης φωτός · Πλήρωμα μυστήριον.
Σοφία τοῦ Θεοῦ · Δύναμις γεωμετρίας Κυρίου.
Γνῶσις τῆς ἀληθείας · Δύναμις γεωμετρίας Κυρίου.
Ἰησοῦς ὁ λειτουργὸς τῶν μυστηρίων.

It must here be noted that ἡ μυστικὴ σοφία = 1767,
representing a higher geometrical function of the
μυστήριον 1178 which is twice the πεντέρημα 589, or
Five-word mystery of the ἔνδυμα or Robe of Jesus,
and 1178 + 589 = 1767. This has already been dealt
with in our " Preliminary Investigation" where its dis-
covery in the Pistis Sophia is mentioned and described
under the name Μυστήριον Πεντέρημα, 1767. As it will
occur again, some account of its geometry seems called
for here, and we trust we may render it intelligible.

In conventional mathematical tables there will usually
be found some facts concerning the five Regular Solids.
These are (1) the Tetrahedron, bounded by four equi-
lateral triangles: the Octahedron, bounded by eight
of the same: and the Cube, bounded by six squares,
whilst the remaining two regular Solids, the Dodecahedron

and the Eikosihedron do not now concern us. The first three are beautifully related in a manner which may easily be shown by the construction of an outline or hollow model in which the Cube may be seen to contain two Tetrahedra interpenetrating and forming, as it were, a Star of eight points, each point being in itself a smaller and perfect Tetrahedron.

Now each of the larger Tetrahedra occupies one-third of the solidity of the Cube which contains them, but as they intersect, there is a central part which is common to both, and this centre is a perfect Octahedron. The Octahedron is exactly one-sixth of the solidity of the Cube. Hence, as it belongs to both Tetrahedra, and the solidity of each of these is one-third of the Cube, the conjoint solidity of the two must be two-thirds of the Cube, less the value of the Octahedron in centre, which we must not count twice over, as it is common to both.

So the solidity of the Star must be $\frac{2}{3} - \frac{1}{6}$ or $\frac{1}{2}$, *i.e.* the Star occupies exactly one-half of the solid bulk of the Cube.

Now this eight-pointed Star is completely hidden within the Cube, only its edges being traced upon the six faces of the Cube, and these edges lie across the diagonals of those six faces, making a cross in each of the six squares. This is of course equally true for all Cubes, but there are two Cubes principally which will claim our attention.

The first of these is the Cube whose edges measure 1,000,—1, 10, or 100—it does not matter greatly, but let us say the measure is 1. Then the length of each cross line or diagonal on the faces is the root of two, given in the Tables as 1·4142. So 1·4142 becomes the length of each edge of the enclosed Tetrahedra. When we come to deal with the gematria of the Star in the East, we shall be able to show that this system of measurement is aimed at, and that it leads to the consideration of another figure in higher space which is the parent figure of the Tetrahedron, the reality of which the Tetrahedron is but an earthly shadow: and this higher figure is a Star of five points instead of four, so that the double of this will give us a Star of ten points.

Now as to the second of the Cubes, which for the moment principally concerns us. This is the Cube which contains a Tetrahedron whose edge is 1. So the edge of the containing Cube must now be reduced to the half of the square root of two, which is 0·7071. This we note was incorrectly stated in our previous book, and we take this opportunity of making the correction. The Tetrahedron in this Cube has then an edge measuring 1·00 and a solidity or solid content of 0·117859, etc. This fraction will be found to be one-twelfth of the Root of two.

But the solid content of our second Cube is $(0·7071)^3$ and this is 0·3535 and as we have seen, the Tetrahedron is one-third of the Cube, so that 1178 stands for one-third of the Cube 353 or 354. In the conventional gematria the value 354 is generally taken as representing this Cube, and following the teaching in the XVIIth Clementine Homily, where St. Peter is supposed to instruct us that the Cube is the form of God, we see the reason why, since 354* is in gematria Ο Θεὸς = God. As for the other, the tetrahedral measure, ordinary mathematical tables give it as 0·1178, and with this the gematria usually agrees in Gnostic use. For example, St. Irenaeus has kindly preserved for us the phrase implying the hollow form of the Tetrahedron, namely Σκία καὶ κένωμα (= Outline and Void space), with the number 1178. This again is the number of Μυστήριον,

---

* This is the Cube Ὠμέγα, since the perimeter of its edges 12 × ·7071 = 84·852, by convention 849 = Ὠμέγα. Its surface is 3 or 6 × 0·5 = $(6 × [·7071]^2)$. When the *Tessaract* = 849⁰⁰, the corresponding Pen-terema = 1767.

the regular Gnostic term for this solid. But those who used this convention knew well that it was rather under the true calculus, and they sometimes made it 1179 as the Α′ Μυστήριον or Alpha Mystery.

And now we come to the higher calculus, to which these geometrical figures lead and point. There is a mathematical equivalent of the Cube in what we term the "fourth dimension," and we can get the value of this by multiplying by the fourth power. Where the edge is 0·7071, the fourth power must be 0·2500. In gematria this appears as 2500 = Φῶς Κυρίου—Light of the Lord. Φῶς is always the typical mystery-word in use when dealing with the higher space as the source of all spiritual enlightenment. 2500 is also Δύναμις ἐκ τοῦ Κυρίου and Λόγος τῆς σωτηρίας.

But our old geometricians seem not to have been quite convinced of the measure 0·7071, or, if they were, at least they seem to have preferred to employ the convention 707.* Consequently when calculating the value of the Tessaract, or higher-spaced figure based on this cube of 354, the "Cube of God," they took the fourth power of 7·07, which is, by gematria, 2498, and on this they build the expression Γνῶσις Θεοῦ Πατρός. Or, as doubtless preferred by some, the value 2499 (Γεωμετρία Θεοῦ Πατρός).

Now we feel some confidence in the assumption that St. Luke or his authority in ch. iv, if consciously involving this geometrical teaching, elected to choose as his basis for the Higher Power of the Cube of God, the value 2498, and we will give our reason.

There is a wonderful fact to be mentioned in connection with the higher powers of the Tetrahedron and the Cube of equal edges. They are not, as in the lower spaces of Plane and Solid, incommensurable, but for

---

* Ἑρμῆς ὁ Θεός.
  353 + 354 = 707.

the first time, *integrally related*, the higher content of the Tetrahedral figure, or Penterema, being exactly one-forty-eighth part of the Tessaract. Thus to get the value of the Penterema which corresponds to the Tessaract on the Cube of God, we must divide 2498 by 48. See the result!

$\dfrac{48/2498 \cdot 00}{52 \cdot 04}$. And as 5204 this great Mystery is expressed. The Tetrahedron is the symbol of Cosmos, of the physical order, and the way of escape from this is by the attainment of the initiate to a knowledge of the Fifth Point and its direction, and the vision of the Penterema, the mystery of the Five Words embroidered on our Lord's Robe of Light, will direct him towards the realisation of That which is beyond all earthly limitations, and which is the treasury of all spiritual powers. Christ is the Open Door ἡ ἀνεῳγμένη θύρα = 1480 Χριστός — He is the Stone (or Cube) of Three Infinite dimensions — Λίθος τρισεπάπειρος = 1480, and when the Cube is 14800 the Penterema is 3083 = the volume of the Penterema whose edge is 40·00. And Χριστός is 40 × 37.

So ὁ Διεληλυθὼς · Μεσσίας ὁ Σωτήρ = 3700.

Now for awhile let us follow the narrative of the mysteries as given in the Pistis Sophia. It tells a glorious story of our Lord's ascension, and how, when the time of His ministry was accomplished, He sat with His disciples on the Mount of Olives, which mount, τὸ ὄρος τῶν ἐλαίων 2856, is by interpretation Μυστήριον Σωτῆρος, and, in the Clementine Homily already mentioned, Τὸ ἄνω · Τὸ κάτω · Ἡ καρδία,—ascent and descent in space, with another and inward motion. And when sitting with the disciples, it was borne to His mind that He had not yet received His Robe of Light. (Ἔνδυμα Κυρίου = 1500 = Φῶς), which He had left when He descended to earth among men. But while the disciples watched, there descended a mighty Light (Μέγα φῶς = 1549 = Τὸ Α′ Μυστήριον) which enveloped Him, and He arose into the heights. But after a while, returning, He told what had befallen. First, He had seen in His robe, a mystery written in Five Words, words which appertained to the height. These words are given as Ζαμα Ζαμα Ὤζζα Ραχαμα Ὤζαι, and the gematria of the phrase is 2474, and this is 1767 + 707. It will be unnecessary for us to emphasise the nature and meaning of these figures so characteristic of the mysteries we have been discussing. It only remains to be shown that, as a total, they contain the same allusion to the measure of the Cube of God. For 2474 stands for Seven Times the solidity of that Cube (353·5).

The story goes on to narrate how Jesus tells of His flight into the height, and how He reached the Gates of the Firmament, blazing with light so bright that the Archons of the Gates could see nothing but the radiance of the Robe and the Mystery of their own order upon it. The Lord Himself they saw not. They trembled, and chanted hymns to the Inmost of the Inmost, and perforce they let Him through the gates. One need not here pause to discriminate between the Gate and its Doors, but ἡ πύλη τοῦ στερεώματος—the Gate of the Firmament 3317 in gematria, is the Gate that leads from our own three-dimensional Space to that unimaginable Next, and the phrase given has a gematria worthy of study. 3317, for example, stands for the following :—

3317 = Ἰησοῦς τὸ Πλήρωμα Κυρίου.
     Jesus, the Fulness of the Lord.
     Ὁ Χριστὸς, Κύριος τῆς Βασιλείας.
     Christ, Lord of the Kingdom (1767).
     Χριστὸς ἡ Θύρα · Ἡ Ὁδὸς τῆς Βασιλείας.
     Christ the Gate : the Way of the Kingdom.

Ὁδὸς τῆς σοφίας Θεοῦ Κυρίου.
Way of the Wisdom of the Lord God.

Θήσαυρος βασιλείας φωτός.
Treasury of the Kingdom of Light.

Ἰησοῦς Λόγος · Χριστὸς Πνεῦμα.
Jesus (the) Word : Christ (the) Spirit.

Ὁ Ὤν · Ὁ Ἦν · Ὁ Ἐρχόμενος · Πλήρωμα.
He Who Is, Was, and Shall Be : the Fulness.

Ὁ αἰώνιος Θεὸς Παντοκράτωρ.
The Eternal God Almighty.

In the viiith chapter of St. John's Gospel is the bold declaration of the Lord " Before Abraham was, I am " —πρὶν Ἀβραὰμ γενέσθαι ἐγὼ εἰμι = 1541. This number yields some striking phrases :—

1541 = Τὸ Α · τὸ Ω.
The First : the Last.

Α · Ω · ὁ ἐπὶ πασὶ Θεός.
First : Last : God over All.

Α καὶ Ω · Ἀρχή.
First and Last : Beginning.

Ὁ Ἦν · Ὁ Θεὸς · Πατρότης.
Who Was : God : Fatherhood.

Ὁ Ἦν · Ὁ Θεὸς · Πλήρωμα.
Who Was : God : Fulness.

Ὁ Ἦν · Ὁ Θεὸς · Μέγας παράκλητος.
Who Was : God : Great Paraclete.

Ἀίδιος Κυρίος · Τὸ Εἶναι.
Eternal Lord : Being.

Ἀίδιος Λόγος · Ἐγὼ εἰμι.
Eternal Word : " I am."

Αἴδιος Θεὸς · Τριὰς τελεία.
Eternal God : Perfect Trinity.

Θεὸς · Θεὸς · Θεὸς · Ἡ Οὐσία.
God (in three Persons) : Substance.

Κύβος · { Ἡ Μονὰς ἐν τριάδι.
      { Ἡ Τριὰς ἐν Μονάδι.

A Cube : { Three in One.
      { One in Three.

It is tempting to suggest the reading πρὶν ἤ in the text under consideration. This would make the gematria 1549 (τὸ Α' μυστήριον).

But we know of no "various reading" in this instance, and the text, as it stands, is better.

The doctrine of the Holy Trinity is older than theologians are apt to regard it. The geometrical figure of the Cube, with its three Dimensions or ἄπειρα, and the three faces or πρόσωπα of the Stone or metacubic figure, may well claim greater antiquity as a symbol of the Deity than the times of Clement. The τρία ἄπειρα κύβου have the gematria 1500, again Φῶς; and even the number of God ὁ Θεὸς 354 is only a variant of the 353 of the Hermetic divinity (Ἑρμῆς), whose three aspects or persons, as we may easily infer from the gematria appear in the Christian system as 353 + 353 + 353* = 1059, the Fatherhood, Fulness, and Great Paraclete as already explained. And it would seem indeed that the name Apollo (Ἀπόλλων = 1061) is but a rather more accurate count of the same, since 1061 = 3 × 353·6, one-fourth of 1414·4.

We now approach another Miracle of Escape, the passage running thus:—"But Jesus was hidden, and went out of the Temple." It may be noted that ἐκρύβη is passive, and not the middle "hid Himself."

Ἰησοῦς δὲ ἐκρύβη καὶ ἐξῆλθεν ἐκ τοῦ ἱεροῦ   = 3010

for which we may read:—

3010 = Θησαυρός τοῦ μείζονος κόσμου.
        Treasury of the Greater Universe.
        Σφαῖρα Κυρίου · Θύρα κεκρυμμένη.
        Sphere of the Lord : Hidden Door.
        Ὁ λόγος + Μυστήριον Πεντέρημα κεκρυμμένον.
        The Word : Hidden Five-word Mystery.

---

* Ἑρμῆς 353 = $4^4 + 3^4 + 2^4$.
  Ὁ Θεὸς 354 = $4^4 + 3^4 + 2^4 + 1^4$.

In the beginning was the Word, or Κύριος ὁ Λόγος
+ 1767.

And the very stones seem to cry the mystery. "They
took up stones to cast at Him"

Ἦραν οὖν λίθους ἵνα βάλωσιν ἐπ᾽ αὐτὸν   = 3458

which may be interpreted

3458 = Μυστήριον κεκρυμμένον · Ἡ ἀνεῳγμένη Θύρα.
      Hidden Mystery : The Open Door
and ἡ ἀνεῳγμένη θύρα = 1480 = Χριστὸς.

The next passage to be quoted is from St. John x, 39,
where again the Lord claims to be the Christ, and Son
of God.   On this occasion "they sought again to take
Him, but He escaped from their hand."

Ἐξήτουν οὖν πάλιν αὐτὸν πιάσαι · καὶ ἐξῆλθεν ἐκ τῆς
χειρὸς αὐτῶν—"They sought again to take Him, but
He escaped from their hand."

The whole gematria of this passage, including the οὖν
omitted by the Revisers, is 5921 on which we find some
interesting combinations, such as :—

Τὸ ἔσω μυστήριον Ἰησοῦ Χριστοῦ Κυρίου.
The Inward Mystery of the Lord Jesus Christ.
Λόγος Φωτός · ᾽Ανάληψις Κυρίου σωτῆρος.
Word of Light : Ascension of the Lord the Saviour.
Λόγος Φωτός · πλήρωμα σωτηρίας Κυρίου.
Word of Light : Fulness of the Salvation of the
      Lord.
Ἡ δύναμις Ἰησοῦ Χριστοῦ · ἡ δύναμις τῆς σωτηρίας.
The Power of Jesus Christ : the Power of Salvation.
Μυστήριον Φωτός · κεκρυμμένον Πεντέρημα Κυρίου
      Θεοῦ.
Mystery of Light : Hidden Five-word (Mystery)
      of the Lord God,

or

Τὸ Φῶς Θεοῦ Κυρίου · κεκρυμμένον μυστήριον πεντέρημα.

But the genuine intent of the text is obviously contained in the latter half of the passage "but He escaped from their hand."

This enumerates at 3267 and it will at once be seen that here we have a remarkable number in the geometry of the Higher Spaces. For 3267 is 1500+1767—in fact it is

$$\Phi\tilde{\omega}\varsigma \cdot \text{Μυστήριον Πεντέρημα}$$

and, for the convenience of readers, we would recall the fact that $\dfrac{1767}{1500}$ is precisely $1\cdot178$. No number, we think, could be more truly expressive of the Mystery of the Tetrahedron and its higher counterpart. Had we wished to express this, such a number would have been that which we should have chosen.

Again in 5921 we discern a mystical value of the higher symmetries, for when a Penterema has a hypersolidity of 592 the corresponding Cube is to be expressed as 284 or 2841, and 284 = Θεός—God. And 592 is Θεότης—Deity, or Godhead.

One great example remains, which perhaps can scarcely be grouped as a miracle of escape, and should stand by itself though it may be included in this chapter, at least to the extent that it confirms the theological mathematics that have been indicated. When our Lord on the First Easter Day had broken The Bread at Emmaus as He sat at meat with those two disciples He vanished from their sight

Καὶ αὐτὸς ἄφαντος ἐγένετο ἀπ᾿ αὐτῶν.

31+971 +1122   +438+81+1551=4194.

This number is the sum of 927+3267=4194.   927 is ὁ Λόγος Θεοῦ, or that title of Christ which the Gnostic Book adopts ὁ Ζῶν, He that liveth.   And 3267 is the 1500+1767 which has been already given, Φῶς · μυστήριον Πεντέρημα.

But there is more on 4194.

      Ἐξουσία τοῦ Κυρίου σωτῆρος,   = 4194.
      Power of the Saviour Lord.

      Τὸ Πνεῦμα ἅγιον · Ἐξουσία Ἰησοῦ Χριστοῦ, = 4194,
and most significantly,

      Εὐχαριστία, μυστήριον Πεντέρημα κεκρυμμένον.
        1627   + 1767   + 800 = 4194.
      Δύναμις Μυστηρίου · θύρα τῆς βασιλείας Θεοῦ.
        705   + 1528 + 510 + 508   + 459 + 484
                                      = 4194.

The connection of the Eucharistic elements with the teaching of these mystical mathematics in the Bruce Codex and in the Pistis Sophia is very plain. This will need separate attention, as the formula points to spherical geometry carried into higher space.

      Ἡ σοφία + ἡ εὐχαριστία τοῦ Κυρίου.
        789   + 1635   + 1770   = 4194.
      Ἡ ἀποκεκρυμμένη σοφία τῆς γνώσεως.
        8   + 839   + 781 + 508 + 2058   = 4194.

The case of Philip the Deacon must be mentioned. The text however is somewhat perplexing. Though St. Luke met Philip and probably got most of the earlier history from him, the actual text seems to have suffered much at the hands of ecclesiastics to whom Philip's proceedings must have appeared very uncanonical, and much too summary. One reading states that the Spirit descended on the eunuch and an angel of the Lord caught away Philip. But the passage as it stands is

      The Spirit of the Lord caught away Philip.
      Πνεῦμα Κυρίου ἥρπασεν τὸν Φίλιππον.
        576 + 1000   + 444 + 420   + 830   = 3270,
or

      Φῶς τοῦ Κυρίου   = 3270.

  Again

      Φίλιππος δὲ εὑρέθη εἰς Ἄζωτον   = 2959.

Now this is one of the most direct suggestions of a carrying of the physical body out of " space," that we meet with in Scripture, and the gematria is a plain intimation of the change in the material constitution by which this process becomes possible. For

$$\text{'H } \mu\epsilon\tau\epsilon\nu\sigma\omega\mu\acute{a}\tau\omega\sigma\iota\varsigma = 2959,$$

and also

$$\text{'H } \gamma\nu\tilde{\omega}\sigma\iota\varsigma \text{ K}\nu\rho\acute{\iota}o\nu \text{ 'I}\eta\sigma o\tilde{\nu},$$

for only by that higher knowledge of cosmic laws could this possibility be achieved. It is the knowledge, again, of the higher space, and is symbolised by the fifth point of the Penterema figure. So

$$\text{T}\grave{o} \ \pi\epsilon\nu\tau\acute{\epsilon}\rho\eta\mu a = 959$$

is the authority
that controls

$$\text{'E}\xi o\nu\sigma\acute{\iota}a \ \tau o\tilde{\nu} \ \Theta\epsilon o\tilde{\nu} = 2000$$

$$\overline{2959.}$$

The problem to be solved is really this: Assuming for the sake of argument that living and other bodies can be made to disappear from one place and re-appear elsewhere, or, if that be too large an assumption, then if we assume that they were thought to be capable of such movement, can the mathematical theory of this phenomenon be shown to have been reasonably attempted?—and with what success in the way of demonstrating that assumption? In regard to the Coptic Gnostic books, the attempt, at least, is clear. Nothing but geometry, and geometry of no ordinary sort, can be implied by certain phrases found therein. But the right of those authors to claim for our Lord's teaching a geometrical basis needs to be substantiated, and this can be done to a very great extent from Scripture itself. St. John and the author of the Epistle to the Hebrews each starts his work by saying outright that all things were created by Him Who is Christ the Lord. And Creation includes things invisible, and

"Aeons" or worlds. But the word "Aeon" is a term very difficult to define or to determine. There is an element of Time in it, because we have such expressions as προαίωνιος, *i.e.* before the aeons, and also we have "this aeon" and "the aeon to come." But with all this, there is the suggestion or idea present in the word of Things Eternal and everlastingly persistent: that is to say, that in all places as in all times, the aeonial things typified in geometry, or expressed in mathematics, such as the circle and the square, the sphere and the cube, retain their characteristic properties unaffected, properties which seem inherent in Space and essentially immutable.

Yet, by the hypothesis of Creation, these things must have had their birth—otherwise there are Things Uncreate, and the universal statement in St. John i must be defined as applying to the objective counterparts only of Things eternally existent in the realm of Idea. But if Space and Time are but forms of Thought contingent on the existence of the brain of the thinker, then these aeonial verities as far as their geometrical expression is concerned, are results of Creation. The Gospel teaching would seem to be that the most immutable and imperishable things known to Man are part of Creation, but it is clear that to man's intellect the essential nature of things is and must be, hidden, and we are dealing with the objective forms of thought which are liable to modification with the changes in our own cerebral organism. Lately there has been a suggestion made that certain astronomical phenomena demand for their explanation the hypothesis of "a warping of Space." This is congruous with the Gnostic idea, in this way. If a rectilinear body be warped, the warped part leaves its line or linear support. If a plane body be warped, the warped part is out of plane. If a space be warped, the warped part will be out of space—that is to say, Space, as we know it, would be unaccountably modified by the warping, and things in that part of space would disappear because they have been carried out of the three dimensions into a region of which we know nothing. But if a portion of space has disappeared, the points in the unaltered space around will yet in some cases seem to have changed their positions. The "gate of the higher space" would be anywhere where such warping might have taken place, and the Archons of Space—that is, the apparently immutable canons of geometry—would be powerless. So with the narrative of our Lord's ascension through the heights. All the wisdom, the mystery, of the Archons was there, but it was powerless to prevent the progress through the gates. The Tetrahedra Five shone on His robe as mysteries of the Aeon of this world, but the Light, of which they were but the outward framework, was there also, dazzling and resplendent.

Such, seemingly, was the Gnostic idea. God, as the Lord, created Things that pass the understanding of men and angels, celestial archetypes which are translated into forms of cosmic order. These forms pass, but their aeonial prototypes, the generative powers and functions, remain.

MIRACLES IN
THE ACTS OF THE APOSTLES.

This series may be concluded with the mention of six miracles from the Acts of the Apostles, which are miracles of healing corresponding closely with those already given.   Each is accompanied by a short speech or Word of Power.   And for this reason they are selected.   There are of course other records of miracles, such as the signs and wonders reported by St. Paul and St. Barnabas before the Apostles and Elder Brethren at Jerusalem, or the miracles of St. Paul at Ephesus, and others more specific but unaccompanied by words. There are also the stories of Ananias and Sapphira, and of Elymas, which are of a different type, and so forth. These six are :—

> The healing of the lame man at the Beautiful
>   Gate.
> The healing of Æneas.
> The raising of Tabitha.
> The healing of the cripple at Lystra.
> The casting out of the Python-spirit at Philippi.
> The raising of Eutychus at Troas.

St. Peter and St. John jointly performed the first apostolic miracle, though St. Peter is the spokesman. It seems that the cripple at the Temple Gate took no notice at first of these two worshippers, whom he might have known to be of what may be called the Religious Order of the Poor, or Ebionim.   That is another subject : but when St. Peter said "Look on us" the man thought he might be mistaken.   St. Peter explained that so it was, and then gave the Word of Power, Acts iii, 6. "In the name of Jesus Christ of Nazareth [rise up and] walk."

Ἐν τῷ ὀνόματι Ἰησοῦ Χριστοῦ τοῦ Ναζωραίου
55 + 1100 + 541 + 688 + 1680 + 770 + 1439
περιπάτει.
+ 591 = 6864.

The Revisers omit the words ἔγειραι καὶ (165) and the above is their Greek. And basing our interpretation of the gematria of this passage on the sense which appears to us the most probable, namely, an assertion of the true Authority of the Apostles to do works in the Name of Jesus Christ, we give the following :—
6864 + 165 = 7029.

The Power according to the Mystery of Jesus Christ the Saviour.

Ἡ δύναμις κατὰ μυστήριον Ἰησοῦ Χριστοῦ τοῦ Σωτῆρος.
713 + 1500 + 2368 + 2448
= 7029.

Peter the rock : Light according to the Mystery : Power of the Lord.

Κηφᾶς ὁ Πέτρος· Φῶς κατὰ μυστήριον·Δύναμις τοῦ Κυρίου.
1554 + 3000 + 705 + 1770
= 7029.

John : Fulness of the Lord : The power of Jesus Christ.

Ἰωάννης· Πλήρωμα τοῦ Κυρίου·Ἡ δύναμις Ἰησοῦ Χριστοῦ.
1119 + 1059 + 1770 + 713 + 2368
= 7029.

John and Simon Peter : Powers of the Authority of Jesus Christ.

Ἰωάννης καὶ Σίμων Πέτρος · Δυνάμεις ἐξουσίας Ἰησοῦ
1119 + 31 + 1100 + 755 + 710 + 946 + 688
Χριστοῦ Κυρίου.
+ 1680 + 1000 = 7029

or, omitting the value of the words ἔγειραι καί,

Light according to the Mystery : Gnosis of the Lord's Apostles.

Φῶς κατὰ μυστήριον · γνῶσις ἀποστόλων Κυρίου.
3000 + 1263 + 1601 + 1000 = 6864.

It will be noted that the whole number 7029 reproduces the digits of Κηφᾶς = 729.

ÆNEAS.

In the 9th chapter of the Acts there is a marked break at the end of verse 30, where St. Paul, in danger of his life, is sent back to Tarsus, and the history turns to St. Peter, and to the events that led up to his conversion, an event scarcely less important than the conversion of St. Paul. Two miracles are recorded by him. First he finds at Lydda a man of the name of Αἰνέας (not spelt Αἰνείας as in the classics) who has been paralysed eight years and lies on a bed (κράββατος) which recalls an important miracle of the Lord. The apostle says to him (without any recorded preliminaries) "Æneas, Jesus Christ maketh thee whole, arise and make thy bed." This is rather an odd phrase. Perhaps it might be freely rendered "Arise, and next time you need your bed you can put it for yourself where you will." There is a strong reminder of the Lord's words "Arise, take up thy bed and go unto thy house." And so it may appear when the gematria is studied. Already on three occasions in the Gospel history where paralytics were healed the forgiveness of sins is mentioned. So here apparently. In the Greek there is just one small point in the text to be noted. The older text, Stephanus and the Authorised Version, puts in the article before Χριστός. The Revisers omit it. In this case we venture to use it.

Αἰνέα, ἰᾶται σε Ἰησοῦς ὁ Χριστός.
67 +322+205 +888 +70 +1480   = 3032.
Ἀνάστηθι καὶ στρῶσον σεαυτῷ.
579 +31 +1720 +1706   = 3036.
        ―――――
        6068.

Now 6068 is 37 × 164, or 3700+2368. And it will be noted that this number is divided into two nearly equal moieties, 3032 and 3036. Peter, as the Stone, derives his authority from the Greater Stone (Πέτρος, ὁ λίθος Θεοῦ = 1628 = Κέφαλη γωνίας) Jesus Christ, acknowledged

by him (Acts iv, 11) as Head of the Corner. So we
find the two divisions of this number give us the Two
Powers of the Stone (δυναμεὶς Πέτρου = 1665), the
original and the delegated powers of Salvation, for :—

Κήφας ὁ Πέτρος ὁ σωτήρ   (1554 + 1478) = 3032
and
Κέφαλη γωνίας · Σωτήρ   (1628 + 1408) = 3036.

The intermediate or average value being 3034 or
37 × 82, which stands for the Greater Stone, or Rock,
whence the Stone is hewn. Ἡ μείζων πέτρα · Κέφαλη
γωνίας = 3034, and which again gives the combined
powers :—

Χριστὸς Κύριος ἡ ἐξουσία   = 3034.
Χριστὸς + Κῆφας ὁ Πέτρος   = 3034.
Μάθησις τοῦ Πέτρου · Ἡ μεγάλη ἐξουσία   = 3034.

But the Mystery of Peter the Stone, that is Cephas

Τὸ μυστήριον Κηφᾶ Πέτρου   = 3032
is also the Mystery of the Lord God

Τὸ μυστήριον Θεοῦ Κυρίου   = 3032
just as Μυστήριον Σιμώνος = 2548 is Τὸ μυστήριον Κυρίου
= 2548.

But the total gives another result which seems
simply amazing, for 6068 divides into 2516 + 3552.

Τέκνον ἀφίενταί σου αἱ ἁμαρτίαι.

495   + 877 + 670 + 11 + 463   = 2516
and 3552 is a multiple of 37, standing for

Υἱὸς ἀληθινὸς, πρωτότοκος Θεοῦ   = 3552.

The problem of the reading ἀφίενται or ἀφέωνται
comes in here, as also the already mentioned insertion
or omission of ὁ.

TABITHA.

The other miracle done by St. Peter was done privately
and alone. In this case it is specially mentioned that
it was a disciple, a Christian, who was dead, Tabitha
or Dorcas. St. Peter was sent for, but found on arrival
that all the good people were mourning her as dead,
and following the Lord's example, he turned them out

of the room, and knelt in prayer. Then he simply said "Tabitha, arise."

Ταβιθά ἀνάστηθι. 323 + 579 = 902.

This number, but for a phrase preserved to us by St. Irenæus, must have proved utterly baffling. It would have been an exception which would have seriously damaged the hypothesis. But St. Irenæus tells us of a six-letter name ὄνομα ἐξαγράμματον, which is ΙΗΣΟΥΣ, and the number of ὄνομα ἐξαγράμματον is 902.*

It will be noticed that the name of six letters so corresponds with the Person that the pronoun ὅς which follows it is masculine.

The quotation is this (Irenæus I, viii, 13, Harvey p. 149):

Πρὶν μὲν οὖν, φησὶ, τούτου τοῦ ὀνόματος τὸ ἐπίσημον φανῆναι, τουτέστι τὸν Ἰησοῦν, τοῖς υἱοῖς [τὸν υἱὸν], ἐν ἀγνοίᾳ πολλῇ ὑπῆρχον οἱ ἄνθρωποι. Ὅτε δὲ ἐφανερώθη τὸ ἐξαγράμματον ὄνομα, ὃς σάρκα περιεβάλλετο, ἵνα εἰς τὴν αἴσθησιν τοῦ ἀνθρώπου κατέλθῃ, ἔχων ἐν ἑαυτῷ αὐτὰ τὰ ἓξ καὶ τὰ εἰκοσιτέσσαρα, τότε γνόντες αὐτὸν ἐπαύσαντο τῆς ἀγνοίας, ἐκ θανάτου δὲ εἰς ζωὴν ἀνῆλθον, τοῦ ὀνόματος αὐτοῖς ὁδοῦ γεννηθέντος πρὸς τὸν πατέρα τῆς ἀληθείας.

For, they say, before the six-number of this name appeared to His children, men were in great ignorance. But when the six-letter name appeared, He that clothed Himself in flesh that He might descend to man's perception, having in Himself these very numbers, the Six and the Twenty-four,† then knowing Him, they ceased from their ignorance because the name became to them a way to the Father of Truth.

Notes. Τὸ ἐπίσημον appears to be the name of the Vau or digamma, standing for the number Six in the numeral use of the alphabet.

---

* Note that τὸ ὄνομα ἐξαγράμματον = 1272 = ἡ γεωμετρία.

† *i.e.* 888 = 24 × 37.

Τὸν υἱὸν in the Greek is Hippolytus' variant on our text—probably more correct, and translatable as "Jesus the Son," ὁ Ἰησοῦς ὁ Υἱός in the nominative, giving the gematria 1708, which with τὸ ἐπίσημον added 833, makes 2541.

Ἡ ἀνάστασις τοῦ κόσμου   = 2541.

Again

Ὁ πατὴρ τῆς ἀληθείας   = 1331

is the same as

Ἰησοῦς ὁ Λόγος   = 1331.

This quotation has been somewhat elaborately treated here, because it affords an instance of the kind of help that St. Irenæus is apt to give. The Gnostics that he attacks in the context appear to have been simply counting letters, υἱός being four, and Χρειστός (so spelt) eight, the six would be intermediate to these. But fragments may be discovered which may be seen to belong to a system which was virtually lost to both disputants. Mysteries do tend to fade out slowly, parts remaining after the meaning has been forgotten.

THE CRIPPLE AT LYSTRA.

St. Paul and St. Barnabas in Lycaonia find at Lystra a man who was a cripple from birth listening to them. St. Paul was speaking and turned that keen gaze of his on the man and saw that he had faith to be healed and called with a loud voice to him "Stand upright on thy feet."

Ἀνάστηθι ἐπὶ τοὺς πόδας σου ὀρθός.

579 + 95 + 970 + 355 + 670 + 449   = 3118.

This will stand for

Ἰησοῦς ἐξουσία Κυρίου Θεοῦ   = 3118.

Τὸ μυστήριον τοῦ κόσμου   = 3118.

The man leaped and walked, the Lycaonians could scarcely be restrained from offering sacrifice to the Apostles as gods, the Jews shortly afterwards stoned St. Paul.

PYTHON.

The miracle at Philippi whereby St. Paul cast out a "spirit of Python" from a slave girl is one of very great interest to-day. The woman would now be termed a trance-speaking medium, or some such name. Whether the words given were always used, or whether they represent the general purport of her cries, it is hard to say, but they are "These men are the servants of the most high God who proclaim unto you (or, 'unto us') the way of salvation." The total of the number (reading ὑμῖν) is very large, being 11094, and quite beyond our powers of conjecture, especially when the utterance is that of a spirit. Such utterances, as already shown, were constantly discouraged by the Lord, and here also by St. Paul. Such testimony, albeit quite real, was not required and might contain implied falsehoods, although from the story it may be clearly inferred that the woman's prophecies had a great reputation for truth. The Greek is :—

$$Οὗτοι \ οἱ \ ἄνθρωποι \ δοῦλοι \ τοῦ \ Θεοῦ \ τοῦ \ ὑψίστου$$
$$850+80 \ \ +1120 \ \ +584+770 \ +484+770 \ +2080$$
$$εἰσίν, \ οἵτινες \ καταγγέλλουσιν \ ὑμῖν \ ὁδὸν$$
$$+275 \ \ +645 \ \ \ \ +1123 \ \ \ \ +500+194$$
$$σωτηρίας.$$
$$+1619 \ \ \ \ \ \ \ \ \ \ \ \ \ \ \ \ =11094.$$

St. Paul was troubled by the persistency of this testimony, and finally turned and said "I charge thee in the name of Jesus Christ to come out of her."

$$Παραγγέλλω \ σοι \ ἐν \ \ τῷ \ ὀνόματι \ Ἰησοῦ \ Χριστοῦ$$
$$1053 \ \ \ +280+55+1100 \ +541 \ \ +688 \ \ +1680$$
$$ἐξέλθειν \ ἀπ' \ αὐτῆς.$$
$$+174+81+909 \ \ \ \ \ \ \ \ \ \ \ \ =6561.$$

This is another large number, but it is a rather striking one. It is the Fourth Power of Nine, 9^4, and as Κήφας is 729 or 9^3, it seems *primâ facie* significant, and this interpretation has been found.

Ἰησοῦς Χριστὸς, Μεσσίας ὁ Σωτὴρ πλήρωμα Κυρίου.
888 +1480 +656 +70+1408 +1059 +1000
$$=6561.$$

EUTYCHUS.

In Acts xx, 7 *sqq.* there is the story of the fall of Eutychus from the window. It is stated that he was taken up dead. But St. Paul went down, fell upon him and embraced him, and then said "Trouble not yourselves for his life is in him," went up again, celebrated the Eucharist, partook of food and went on conversing till the daylight and started for the ship. At that juncture it would seem that those who had taken charge of the lad brought him alive, to their great relief. One is inclined to ask whether, strictly speaking, there was a miracle at all, except in the very colloquial modern use of the word. The lad had fallen from the third floor, and, we might say, was saved from death by a miracle. St. Paul's words might be taken to mean simply what they stated, that the life was in the lad and there was no cause for anxiety. But the Greek of those words is

Μὴ θορυβεῖσθε, ἡ γὰρ ψυχὴ αὐτοῦ ἐν αὐτῷ
48 +810 +8 +104 +1708 +1171 +55 +1501
ἐστίν.
+565   = 5970,
and this has a very good gematria
Μυστήριον Σωτῆρος, ἐξουσία Ἰησοῦ Χριστοῦ.
1178 +1678 +746 +2368 = 5970.

It was a miracle then in the proper sense of the word. For μυστήριον Σωτῆρος see the story of Malchus.

NOTES ON A PASSAGE IN THE SEVENTEENTH CLEMENTINE HOMILY.

It is plainly impracticable to give here any account, however succinct, of the problems involved with the connection of the Flavian family with the earliest history of the Gospel in Rome. But certain facts are quite clear and prominent. A Clemens is third on the list of the Bishops of Rome. An epistle of his is extant and genuine. And beyond this there is a traditional story which probably has some basis in history such as seems to underlie the Acts of Paul Thecla and other similar literature.

There survives in Greek a book called the Clementine Homilies, of which the epitome that is most accessible may be that in Smith's Dictionary of Christian Biography, under the heading "Clementine Literature." And, as that article says, "such a document must be most valuable for the light which it throws on the opinions of the School from which it emanated."

The passage here given is from the Greek text of Albert Schwegler of Tubingen published in 1847 and from Albert Dressel published in 1853. A paraphrase has been attempted, but the text must tell its own story, subject to critical emendation which can scarcely be attempted here.

It is called in evidence on two main points. It shows the character of the teaching attributed to St. Peter when confronted with the pseudonymous gnosis of Simon Magus, who was perhaps the most dangerous enemy that the earlier disciples had to encounter. It assumes that our Lord's meaning in His parables was made known to His Apostles, and that they knew of a way in which the parables could be interpreted. It gives a strong indication of the geometrical character of the interpretation, and makes it plain that St. Peter was regarded as equal to a discussion on the highest philosophical problems that could be debated in his day.

THE SIX BOUNDLESS LINES.
ΤΑ 'ΕΞ 'ΑΠΕΙΡΑ.

St. Peter is challenged to name the place where God is, and he has an answer ready. The place of God is τὸ μὴ ὄν, and the definition is that of the point which is the meeting place of the Six Boundless Lines, which would now be called the Cartesian co-ordinates. The point is zero, no dimension, nor will any multiple of zero have any substance or reality: $x \times 0 = 0$. But the mere assignment of such a place to God is meant to show that He is both within and without space as we know it. And though *primâ facie* there appears a contradiction in calling τὸ μὴ ὄν a place, no contradiction exists because a positive intellectual reality is implied in the idea of a geometrical point or series of points. The point is called a boundary or terminal of all things. And this is used of the inward direction in this case. The six boundless lines meet and stop at the point where God is. So also do eight other boundless lines directed this time not to the centres of the six sides of a cube, but to the eight corners. It will be seen that the six lines divide the cube into eight cubes, each cube meeting the seven others at the central point. Therefore the point, τὸ μὴ ὄν, may be said to be bounded by eight terminal cubes, or conversely to be the common boundary of eight cubes. This is the condition of the hypercube or tessaract. And here seems to be the explanation of the strange phrase Τοῦ ἄνω τε καὶ κάτω δὶς ὑπάρχων καρδία. The point that is the heart of a tessaract as well as of ordinary three dimensional geometry. One can see the tessaract contracted to a point at the junction of the eight cubes, and a point is all that we can visualise of it. The eight lines are of the order of $\sqrt{3}$ and they will be recognised among the lines of the analysed tessaract on p. 85.

It may also be noted that the eight boundless lines divide into two fours as the axes of the interpenetrated tetrahedra and pass through the centres of the eight triangles of the octohedron in the cube. The four $\sqrt{3}$ lines in the cube pass through its substance, as do the two $\sqrt{2}$ lines in the square, and in the tessaract the eight $\sqrt{4}$ lines also pass through the hypercubic substance. Backed by other evidence this passage in the Clementine Homilies seems, certainly to indicate a four-dimensional hypothesis and is worthy of deeper study than this merely exploratory excursus can pretend to.

PARAPHRASE,
CLEMENTINE HOMILIES XVII, VI—X.

St. Peter speaks :—

Our Lord Jesus being a true prophet, as I shall presently disclose more fully, was wont to make His pronouncements concisely when He dealt with crucial matters of the truth, and that for two reasons. First that His words were directed to those who had knowledge requisite for belief in what He said. For what He spoke was not strange to them in matter, or different in style from that to which they had become accustomed.

Secondly, because the time in which He preached was set, and He would not spend it in explanations of things which His hearers could understand if they took the trouble, and so risk the omission of anything crucial. For He revealed such things as He wished as to an audience able to understand, such as we were, and we, whenever, as on rare occasions it happened, we did not understand what He said, ascertained it from Him privately, lest we should lose His meaning.

Knowing therefore that we knew His doctrine and were able to explain it, He sent us to the unlearned Gentiles to baptise them for the remission of sins and to teach them previously the commandments of which the first and great one is to fear the Lord God and worship Him only. But He added that the God to be feared was He whose angels, the angels to wit of the least among the faithful, stood in Heaven always beholding His face.

For God has a form, by reason of His primal and unique beauty, and all limbs, not indeed for use, for He has not eyes in order that He may see, for He sees in every direction being beyond comparison brighter in body than the visualising spirit in us, and more resplendent than all light, so that the sun's light in comparison with His would be counted as darkness. Nor again has God ears in order that He may hear, for He hears from every direction, understands, moves, works, makes.

But God has this most beauteous form for man's sake that the pure in heart may be able to see Him, and that they may rejoice that it was on account of such beauty that they suffered as they did. For He fashioned man to the likeness of His own form, as in the greatest mould, that man might be the ruler and lord of all things and that all things might serve him. Wherefore he that desires to worship God, discerning that the all is God and man God's image, God being invisible, honours God's visible image which in very fact is man. What thing soever therefore that anyone does to man, whether good or evil, is considered as done to God. Wherefore also God's judgment shall go forth on all, awarding to each his just deserts; for God vindicates the honour of His own form.

But someone will say: "If God has Form He also has Fashion and is in a Place. But if in a place then He must be smaller than the place which contains Him, and how can He then be great above all things? And how can He be everywhere being of a Fashion?"

Now to one who so speaks it is possible to answer
thus: "This is what the Scriptures would have us
think and believe about God, but we know that the
Scriptures are true, for our Lord Jesus Christ bore
witness to them, and it is by His command that we
must needs give you the proofs that so it is."

But first I will speak of Place. And the Place of
God is "That-which-is-not," but God is That-which-is.
But That-which-is-not is not comparable with "That-
which-is." For how can that which is a place be said
to exist unless there be a second region, such as
Heaven, earth, water, air or any other such body which
can occupy the space to hold it, which for that very
fact is called empty because it is nothing.* For this,
"The no-thing," is its more suitable designation. For
that which is called empty is anything whatever such
as a vessel which contains nothing except the vessel
itself, which is void, and not a place but that in which
emptiness is, if that be the instance chosen. For by
the very necessity of the case "That-which-is" must
be in That-which-is-not. But this, the That-which-is-
not, is, I say, that which is called Place by some, being
in itself actually nothing. But how is the nothing to
be compared with That-which-is except by contraries,
denying existence to That-which-is and calling That-
which-is-not Place? But if this also be something I will
use just one of the many examples that rush to my
mouth to show that not in every case is the surrounding
medium greater than that which it surrounds. The sun
is of definite fashion and is altogether surrounded by
the air, warms the air, pierces the air, and if it be
absent from the air, the air is shrouded in darkness,
and from whatever part of the air the sun happens to
be absent that part is deadly chilled. But by the
rising of the sun the air is again enlightened, and

* Τὸ μὴ ὂν καί τὸ ὂν = 1059 = πλήρωμα.
Θεὸs + τὸ οὐδὲν = 1183 = κεκρυμμένον σημεῖον.

wheresoever it is warmed by the sun it is adorned with greater beauty. And this the sun does, albeit its substance is within definite limits by its power to communicate. What then hinders God, as being the Maker and Lord of this and all other things, and being Himself in fashion form and beauty, from having His‚ power to communicate infinitely extended?

The very subsisting God is therefore One, Who enthroned· in more excellent form, is the heart dually controlling both that which is above and that which is is below, sending forth from Himself as from a centre the life giving and bodiless power, all things with the stars and regions of Heaven, air, water, earth, fire, and whatever there be aught else, boundless in height, unlimited in depth, immeasured in breadth, thrice to the boundless stretching forth His life-giving and provident nature. This, therefore, that, starting from God, is boundless in every direction, must needs be the heart holding Him Who is verily above all things in fashion, Who, wheresoever He be, is as it were in the middle of a boundless space being the terminal of the All. Taking their origin therefore from Him, the six* extensions have the nature of unlimited things. Of which the one taking its beginning from God is displayed upwards towards the height, another downwards towards the depth, another to the right, another to the left, another in front, another behind. And looking forth on these as on a number equal in every direction, God completes the world in six equal divisions of time, He Himself being the Repose, and having as a likeness the boundless Æon that is to be, God being the Beginning and the End. For at Him the six boundless lines do terminate and from Him they take their boundless extension.

---

* Schwegler and Dressel print ἐξ from an accented MS. Why not ἕξ. The MS. need not be faultless. See the Greek. An asterisk marks the passage.

This is the mystery of the week.   For God Himself
is the Repose of the Whole, just as He grants a Repose
to those who imitate in miniature some great act of
His own.   He is Alone, apprehensible at any place, but
having His extensions to the boundless.   For this God
is apprehensible and inapprehensible, near and far, here
and there, as being by nature the Only one.   And by
the partaking in the power of His mind boundless in
every direction, by which the souls of all do breathe,
they have life.   And even if they be separated from
the body and are found to possess the desire that
yearns for Him, they are borne to His bosom, as in
the winter time the mists of the mountains, drawn by
the rays of the sun are borne towards it, immortal.
What a love then are we able to gain if we apprehend
with the mind the fair form of God!   Otherwise it is
impracticable.   For it is impossible that beauty should
exist without form, or that anyone should be drawn
to the love of God, or think to see God, had God no
similitude.

Ἀληθὴς ὢν προφήτης ὁ κύριος ἡμῶν Ἰησοῦς Χριστός, ὡς ἐπὶ
καιροῦ καὶ περὶ τούτου πληροφορήσω, περὶ τῶν τῇ ἀληθείᾳ
διαφερόντων συντόμως τὰς ἀποφάσεις ἐποιεῖτο, διὰ δύο
ταῦτα, ὅτι πρὸς θεοσεβεῖς ἐποιεῖτο τὸν λόγον, εἰδότας τὰ
ἀποφάσει ὑπ᾽ αὐτοῦ ἐκφερόμενα πιστεύειν· οὐδὲ γὰρ ἦν
ξένα τῆς αὐτῶν συνηθείας τὰ λεγόμενα. δεύτερον δὲ ὅτι
προθεσμίαν ἔχων κηρῦξαι τῷ τῆς ἀποδείξεως οὐκ ἐχρῆτο
λόγῳ, ἵνα μὴ εἰς λόγους τὸν πάντα τῆς προθεσμίας δαπανῷ
χρόνον, καὶ οὕτως αὐτῷ συμβήσεται, εἰς ὀλίγων λόγων ἐπιλύσεις
ἀσχολουμένῳ, τῶν ὑπὸ πόνου ψυχῆς νοεῖσθαι δυναμένων,
τοὺς ἀληθείᾳ διαφέροντας μὴ ἐπὶ πλεῖον εἰσφέρειν λόγους.
ἐπειδὴ περὶ ὧν ἤθελεν ἀπεφαίνετο, ὡς λαῷ νοεῖν δυναμένῳ,
ἀφ᾽ ὧν ἐσμεν καὶ ἡμεῖς, οἳ ὁπότε κατὰ τὸ σπάνιον οὐκ
ἐνοήσαμέν τι τῶν ὑπ᾽ αὐτοῦ ῥηθέντων, ἰδίᾳ ἐπυνθανόμεθα,
μὴ ἡμῖν τι τῶν ὑπ᾽ αὐτοῦ ῥηθέντων ἀνόητον ᾖ.

Εἰδὼς οὖν ἡμᾶς πάντα εἰδότας τὰ ὑπ' αὐτοῦ ῥηθέντα καὶ τὰς ἀποδείξεις παρασχεῖν δυναμένους, εἰς τὰ ἀμαθῆ ἔθνη ἀποστέλλων ἡμᾶς, βαπτίζειν αὐτοὺς εἰς ἄφεσιν ἁμαρτιῶν, ἐνετείλατο ἡμῖν πρότερον διδάξαι αὐτούς· ἀφ' ὧν ἐντολῶν αὕτη πρώτη καὶ μεγάλη τυγχάνει, τὸ φοβηθῆναι κύριον τὸν Θεὸν καὶ αὐτῷ μόνῳ λατρεύειν. Θεὸν δὲ φοβεῖσθαι ἐκεῖνον εἶπεν, οὗ οἱ ἄγγελοι τῶν ἐν ἡμῖν ἐλαχίστων πιστῶν ἐν τῷ οὐρανῷ ἑστήκασι θεωροῦντες τὸ πρόσωπον τοῦ πατρὸς διαπαντός. μορφὴν γὰρ ἔχει, διὰ πρῶτον καὶ μόνον κάλλος καὶ πάντα μέλη, οὐ διὰ χρῆσιν· οὐ γὰρ διὰ τοῦτο ὀφθαλμοὺς ἔχει, ἵνα ἐκεῖθεν βλέπῃ· πανταχόθεν γὰρ ὁρᾷ, τοῦ ἐν ἡμῖν βλεπτικοῦ πνεύματος ἀπαραβλήτως λαμπρότερος ὢν τὸ σῶμα, καὶ παντὸς στιλπνότερος, ὡς πρὸς σύγκρισιν αὐτοῦ τὸ ἡλίου φῶς λογισθῆναι σκότος. ἀλλ' οὐδὲ διὰ τοῦτο ὦτα ἔχει, ἵνα ἀκούῃ, πανταχόθεν γὰρ ἀκούει, νοεῖ, κινεῖ, ἐνεργεῖ, ποιεῖ. τὴν δὲ καλλίστην μορφὴν δι' ἄνθρωπον, ἵνα οἱ καθαροὶ τῇ καρδίᾳ αὐτὸν ἰδεῖν δυνηθῶσιν, ἵνα χαρῶσι δι' ἅ τινα ταῦτα ὑπέμειναν. τῇ γὰρ αὐτοῦ μορφῇ ὡς ἐν μεγίστῃ σφραγῖδι τὸν ἄνθρωπον διετυπώσατο, ὅπως ἁπάντων ἄρχῃ καὶ κυριεύῃ, καὶ πάντα αὐτῷ δουλεύῃ. διὸ κρίνας εἶναι τὸ πᾶν αὐτόν, καὶ τὴν αὐτοῦ εἰκόνα τὸν ἄνθρωπον, αὐτὸς ἀόρατος, ἡ δὲ αὐτοῦ εἰκὼν ὁ ἄνθρωπος ὁρατός, ὁ αὐτὸν σέβειν θέλων τὴν ὁρατὴν αὐτοῦ τιμᾷ εἰκόνα, ὅπερ ἐστὶν ἄνθρωπος. ὅ τι ἂν οὖν τις ποιήσῃ ἀνθρώπῳ, εἴτε ἀγαθὸν εἴτε κακόν, εἰς ἐκεῖνον ἀναφέρεται. διὸ καὶ ἡ ἐξ αὐτοῦ κρίσις πᾶσι κατ' ἀξίαν ἀπονέμουσα ἑκάστῳ προελεύσεται. τὴν γὰρ αὐτοῦ μορφὴν ἐκδικεῖ.

Ἀλλὰ ἐρεῖ τις· εἰ μορφὴν ἔχει, καὶ σχῆμα ἔχει καὶ ἐν τόπῳ ἐστίν· ἐν τόπῳ δὲ ὢν καὶ ὑπ' αὐτοῦ περιεχόμενος ὡς ἥττων, πῶς ὑπὲρ πάντα ἐστὶ μέγας; πῶς δὲ καὶ πανταχῆ εἶναι δύναται, ἐν σχήματι ὤν; πρὸς τὸν ταῦτα λέγοιτα πρῶτον ἔστιν εἰπεῖν· τοιαῦτα περὶ αὐτοῦ αἱ γραφαὶ φρονεῖν πείθουσι καὶ πιστεύειν, ἡμεῖς δὲ ἀληθεῖς γινώσκομεν τὰς ἀποφάσεις μαρτυρουμένας ὑπὸ τοῦ κυρίου ἡμῶν Ἰησοῦ Χριστοῦ, οὗ κατὰ κέλευσιν τὰς ἀποδείξεις ὑμῖν τοῦ οὕτως ἔχειν ἀνάγκη παρέχειν. πρῶτον δὲ περὶ τόπου ἐρῶ. καὶ Θεοῦ τόπος ἐστὶ τὸ μὴ ὄν, Θεὸς δὲ τὸ ὄν· τὸ δὲ μὴ ὄν

τῷ ὄντι οὐ συγκρίνεται. πῶς γὰρ τόπος ὢν εἶναι δύναται;
ἐκτὸς εἰ μὴ δευτέρα χώρα εἴη, οἷον οὐρανός, γῆ, ὕδωρ, ἀήρ,
καὶ εἰ ἄλλο τί ἐστι σῶμα, ὃ ἂν καὶ αὐτὸ πληροῖ τὸ
κενόν, ὃ διὰ τοῦτο κενὸν λέγεται, ὅτι οὐδέν ἐστιν. τοῦτο
γὰρ αὐτῷ, τὸ οὐδέν, οἰκειότερον ὄνομα. τὸ γὰρ λεγόμενον
κενόν τί ποτ' ὡς σκεῦός ἐστιν οὐδὲν ἔχον, πλὴν αὐτὸ τὸ
σκεῦος· κενὸν ὂν οὐκ αὐτό ἐστι τόπος, ἀλλ' ἐν ᾧ ἐστὶν
αὐτὸ τὸ κένον, εἴπερ σκεῦός ἐστιν. ἀνάγκη γὰρ πᾶσα τὸ
ὂν ἐν τῷ μηδὲν ὄντι εἶναι. τοῦτο δέ, τὸ μὴ ὄν, λέγω
ὃ ὑπό τινων τύπος λέγεται, οὐδὲν ὄν. οὐδὲν δὲ ὂν τῷ ὄντι
πῶς συγκρίνεται; ἐκτὸς εἰ μὴ ἐν τοῖς ἐναντίοις, ἵνα τὸ μὲν
ὂν μὴ ᾖ, τὸ δὲ μὴ ὂν τόπος λέγηται. εἰ δὲ καὶ ἔστι τι,
πολλῶν παραδειγμάτων σπευδόντων ἐξ ἐμοῦ προελθεῖν
εἰς ἀπόδειξιν ἑνὶ μόνῳ χρήσασθαι θέλω, ἵνα δείξω, ὅτι οὐ
πάντως τὸ περιέχον τοῦ περιεχομένου κρεῖττόν ἐστιν.
ὁ ἥλιος σχῆμά ἐστι περιφερὲς καὶ ὑπὸ ἀέρος ὅλος περιέχεται,
ἀλλὰ τοῦτον ἐκλαμπρύνει, τοῦτον θερμαίνει, τοῦτον τέμνει,
κἂν ἀπῇ αὐτοῦ, σκότῳ περιβάλλεται, καὶ οὗ ἂν αὐτοῦ
μέρους ἀπὼν γένηται, ὡς νεκρούμενον ψύχεται, ὑπὸ δὲ τῆς
αὐτοῦ ἀνατολῆς πάλιν φωτίζεται, καὶ ὅπου ἂν αὐτῷ περι-
θάλπηται, καὶ κάλλει τῷ μείζονι κοσμεῖται. καὶ ταῦτα
ποιεῖ τῇ αὐτοῦ μετουσίᾳ, τὴν οὐσίαν περιωρισμένην ἔχων.
τί οὖν ἔτι κωλύει τὸν Θεόν, ὡς τούτου καὶ πάντων δημιουργὸν
καὶ δεσπότην ὄντα, αὐτὸν μὲν ἐν σχήματι καὶ μορφῇ καὶ
κάλλει ὄντα, τὴν ἀπ' αὐτοῦ μετουσίαν ἀπείρως ἐκτεταμένην
ἔχειν;

Εἷς οὖν ἐστιν ὁ ὄντως Θεός, ὃς ἐν κρείττονι μορφῇ
προκαθέζεται, τοῦ ἄνω τε καὶ κάτω δὶς [καθ]υπάρχων
καρδία, καὶ ἀπ' αὐτοῦ ὥσπερ ἀπὸ κέντρου βρύουσα τὴν
ζωτικὴν καὶ ἀσώματον δύναμιν, τὰ πάντα σύν τε ἄστροις
καὶ νομοῖς οὐρανοῦ, ἀέρος, ὕδατος, γῆς, πυρὸς καὶ εἰ ἄλλο
τί ἐστιν, δείκνυται οὐσία ἄπειρος εἰς ὕψος, ἀπέραντος
εἰς βάθος, ἀμέτρητος εἰς πλάτος, τρισεπάπειρος τὴν
ἀπ' αὐτοῦ ζωοποιὸν καὶ φρόνιμον ἐκτείνουσα φύσιν·
τοῦτο οὖν τὸ ἐξ αὐτοῦ πανταχόθεν ἄπειρον ἀνάγκη
εἶναι καρδίαν, ἔχον τὸν ὄντως ὑπὲρ πάντα ἐν σχήματι,
ὅς, ὅπου πότ' ἂν ᾖ, ὡς ἐν ἀπείρῳ μέσος ἐστίν, τοῦ

παντὸς ὑπάρχων ὅρος. ἀπ᾽ αὐτοῦ οὖν ἀρχόμεναι αἱ ἐκτάσεις ἐξ* ἀπεράντων ἔχουσι τὴν φύσιν. ὧν ὁ μὲν ἀπ᾽ αὐτοῦ λαβὼν τὴν ἀρχὴν διικνεῖται εἰς ὕψος ἄνω, ὁ δὲ εἰς βάθος κάτω, ὁ δὲ ἐπὶ δεξιάν, ὁ δὲ ἐπὶ λαιάν, ὁ δὲ ἔμπροσθεν, ὁ δὲ ὄπισθεν, εἰς οὓς αὐτὸς ἀποβλέπων ὡς εἰς ἀριθμὸν πανταχόθεν ἴσον χρονικοῖς ἐξ διαστήμασι συντελεῖ τὸν κόσμον, αὐτὸς ἀνάπαυσις ὢν καὶ τὸν ἐσόμενον ἄπειρον αἰῶνα εἰκόνα ἔχων, ἀρχὴ ὢν καὶ τελευτή. εἰς αὐτὸν γὰρ τὰ ἐξ ἄπειρα τελευτᾷ, καὶ ἀπ᾽ αὐτοῦ τὴν εἰς ἄπειρον ἔκτασιν λαμβάνει.

Τοῦτό ἐστιν ἑβδομάδος μυστήριον. αὐτὸς γάρ ἐστιν ἡ τῶν ὅλων ἀνάπαυσις, ὃς τοῖς ἐν μικρῷ μιμουμένοις αὐτοῦ τὸ μέγα αὐτὸν χαρίζεται εἰς ἀνάπαυσιν. αὐτός ἐστι μόνος, πῆ μὲν καταληπτός, πῆ δὲ ἀκατάληπτος, πῆ δὲ ἀπέραντος, τὰς ἀπ᾽ αὐτοῦ ἐκτάσεις ἔχων εἰς ἄπειρον. οὕτως γὰρ καταληπτός ἐστι καὶ ἀκατάληπτος, ἐγγὺς καὶ μακράν, ὧδε ὢν κἀκεῖ, ὡς μόνος ὑπάρχων. καὶ διὰ τοῦ πανταχόθεν ἀπείρου νοὸς τὴν μετουσίαν ἔχων, ἣν πάντων ἀναπνέουσαι αἱ ψυχαί, τὸ ζῆν ἔχουσιν· κἂν χωρισθῶσι τοῦ σώματος, καὶ τὸν εἰς αὐτὸν εὑρεθῶσι πόθον ἔχουσαι, εἰς τὸν αὐτοῦ κόλπον φέρονται, ὡς ἐν χειμῶνι ὥρας οἱ ἀτμοὶ τῶν ὀρῶν ὑπὸ τῶν τοῦ ἡλίου ἀκτίνων ἑλκόμενοι φέρονται πρὸς αὐτὸν ἀθάνατοι. οἵαν οὖν στοργὴν συλλαβεῖν δυνάμεθα, ἐὰν τὴν εὐμορφίαν αὐτοῦ τῷ νῷ κατοπτεύσωμεν! ἄλλως δὲ ἀμήχανον. ἀδύνατον γὰρ κάλλος ἄνευ μορφῆς εἶναι, καὶ πρὸς τὸν αὐτοῦ ἔρωτα ἐπισπᾶσθαί τινα, ἢ καὶ δοκεῖν Θεὸν ὁρᾶν εἶδος οὐκ ἔχοντα.

Περὶ τῶν τῇ ἀληθείᾳ διαφερόντων. Compare Rom. ii, 18 and Phil. i, 10. It seems to mean not so much "things that are excellent" but the more important and vital teaching.

Μορφὴ and σχῆμα. Compare Phil. ii, 6. Ὃς ἐν μορφῇ Θεοῦ ὑπάρχων ...... σχήματι εὑρεθεὶς ὡς ἄνθρωπος.

---

* Ref. to note p. 101.

GEMATRIA.

'Η καρδία τῶν ἐξ ἀπείρων   = 2405 = 37 × 65 (65 = ἑξ).
                                    = Φῶς δημιουργός.
                                    = Τὸ ζῶν μυστήριον.

"Καὶ Θεοῦ τόπος ἐστὶ τὸ μὴ
    ὄν, Θεὸς δὲ τὸ ὄν"   = 3071 = 37 × 83.
                                    = Ὁ ἐνεργὴς λόγος · κέντρον
                                        τοῦ κύβου.
                                    = Τὸ τὶ ἦν εἶναι. Κεντρον
                                        τοῦ κύβου.

Θεοῦ τόπος ἐστὶ τὸ μὴ ὄν   = 2257 = 37 × 61.
                                    = Ὠμεγα σωτήρ.
                                      Εὐαγγέλιον Χριστοῦ.
                                      Ὁ θρόνος Κυρίου Ἰησοῦ.
                                      Ο μέγας θησαυρὸς κεκρυμ-
                                        μένος.

Τὰ τῇ ἀληθείᾳ διαφέροντα   = 1714 = 2 × 857 Λόγος Θεοῦ.
                                    = Ζῶν Λόγος Θεοῦ.

Ἔξ ἄπειρα τοῦ κύβου   = 1924 = 37 × 52.
                                    = Ο κόσμος τοῦ Θεοῦ.
                                    Ἡ ἐπιφάνεια τοῦ Θεοῦ.
                                    Αἱ ἐκτάσεις αἱ ἕξ ἀπὸ κέντρου.

Ἔξ ἄπειρα Θεοῦ   = 746 = Ἐξουσία.
Τὸ μὴ ὄν   = 538 = Νόησις. = Ἡ νοητικὴ
                                        ἀλήθεια.

Τόπος Θεοῦ   = 1204 = Νοῦς Θεοῦ.

                              1742 = Ψῆφος Ἀληθείας.

Κέντρον τῶν ἐξ ἀπείρων   = 2856 = Τὸ ἄνω · τὸ κάτω · ἡ
                                    καρδία.
                                    Μυστήριον σωτῆρος.
                                    Ὁ Χριστὸς· μεθ' ἡμῶν ὁ Θεός.

Τόπος Θεοῦ ἀοράτου   = 2146 = 37 × 58.
Τὸ κέντρον τοῦ κύβου   = 2627 = 37 × 71.
Ἡ ἔκτασις τοῦ Θεοῦ   = 1998 = 37 × 54 (6 × 333).
Ἐκτασις τῶν ἐξ ἀπείρων   = 2997 = 37 × 81.

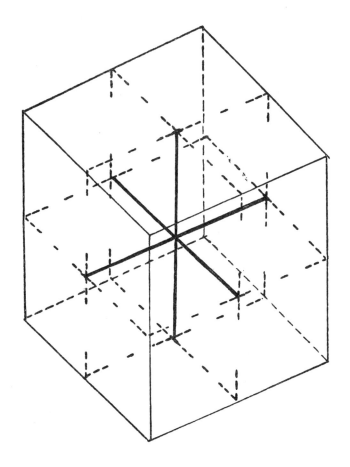

GEOMETRIC INTERPRETATION OF THE FORM OF
GOD DERIVED' FROM THE TEXT OF THE
XVIITH CLEMENTINE HOMILY.

The Six ἄπειρα or Right Lines of infinite extension
are seen to intersect at the Central Point of the Cube,
and they divide the One Cube into Eight lesser Cubes.

Κύβος Κυρίου   'Οκτὼ Κύβοι.
692   +1000 =   1190 +502   =1692.

THE CONFESSION OF ST. PETER.

St. Matthew xvi, 13; St. Mark viii, 27: St. Luke ix, 18.

It would seem that it was in the later summer of the year before His Passion that the Lord went northward beyond the bounds of the land of Israel, setting His face towards the cool heights of Hermon as it were for refreshment from the heat.

On the way was passed the town of Caesarea Philippi, where at the source of the Jordan was a temple built by Herod on a cliff, to the honour of Augustus. And here, after a preliminary question (which is given differently in the three accounts) concerning the opinion of others about Himself, the Lord asks His disciples the further question,—which is given without variation— "But whom say ye that I am?"

῾Υμεῖς δὲ τίνα με λέγετε εἶναι᾽	= 1494,

and on this we find the following:—

῾Η Πέτρα Κυρίου	= 1494.
Ζῶσα πέτρα	= 1494.
῾Ο Μεσσίας τῆς διαθήκης	= 1494.
Μεσσίας ὁ ῞Αγιος Θεοῦ	= 1494.
᾽Εξουσία ἀληθείας Θεοῦ	= 1494.

It is as though Christ, the Living Rock, were anticipating a response from the Stone ὁ πέτρος which is hewn from His mass. Both the Lord and His apostle have the symbol of the Cube.

Christ is the Truth, and Peter the Teaching of the truth on which the Church is built. So the gematria implies most appropriately that the Lord is the ἐξουσία —the Authority—for his teaching.

To this came St. Peter's answer plain at once. St. Matthew and St. Mark give it as "Thou art the Christ," St. Matthew adding, "The Son of the Living God" and also the blessing and commission to St. Peter.

Σὺ   εἶ   ὁ Χριστός.

600 + 15 + 70 + 1480   = 2165.

Which by itself gives

Ὁ ζῶν, ἡ ἐξουσία Θεοῦ   = 2165.

Ὁ Λόγος Θεοῦ, ἡ ἐξουσία Θεοῦ   = 2165.

But there must be added

Ὁ Υἱὸς τοῦ Θεοῦ τοῦ ζῶντος.

70 + 680 + 770 + 484 + 770 + 1427   = 4201

giving by itself

Ἰησοῦς ὁ Λόγος, τὸ φῶς Κυρίου   = 4201

but added to 2165 the number becomes 6366 which
though large, may be thus divided,

2368   Ἰησοῦς Χριστός, etc.

1998   ὁ Υἱὸς ἐκ τῆς παρθένου, etc.

                both being multiples of 37.

2000   Ἐξουσία τοῦ Θεοῦ.

6366

and in many other ways.

The Lord's answer is given by St. Matthew only.

"Blessed art thou Simon Bar Jona."

Μακάριος εἶ Σίμων Βὰρ Ἰωνᾶ,

    442 + 15 + 1100 + 103 + 861   = 2521.

giving,

The Word of God, Simon the Rock.

Ὁ λόγος Θεοῦ Σίμων ἡ πέτρα.

70 + 373 + 484 + 1100 + 8 + 486   = 2521

Peter, the geometry of the Church.

Πέτρος, ἡ γεωμετρία ἐκκλησίας.

    755 + 8   + 1264   + 494   = 2521.

or   Peter: the Rock: the Geometria.

Πέτρος · ἡ πέτρα · ἡ Γεωμετρία.

Simon Peter + 666.

Σίμων Πέτρος + χξϛ'.

1100   + 755 + 666   = 2521.

The last looks very strange.   Yet 666 seems to be
a cosmic and solar symbol and not necessarily evil
except when the world is evil.   The Church has some
power on earth.

For flesh and blood hath not revealed it unto thee.
Ὅτι σὰρξ καὶ αἷμα οὐκ ἀπεκάλυψέν σοι.
$$380 + 361 + 31 + 52 + 490 + 1292 + 280 = 2886.$$

This is a multiple of 37, being 37×78, and may
stand for

Χριστὸς ὁ Υἱὸς Μεσσίας,
Ὁ Σωτήρ, ἡ πέτρα πνευματική,
and others; see the list.

But my Father which is in Heaven.
Ἀλλ᾽ ὁ Πατήρ μου   ὁ ἐν [τοῖς] οὐρανοῖς.
$$61 + 70 + 489 + 510 + 70 + 55 + [580] + 901 = 2166$$
$$\text{or } = 2736.$$

The inclusion of τοῖς is doubtful, but perhaps really
immaterial, for

Μεσσίας + φῶς   = 2156.
Μεσσίας + τὸ Ἅγιον Πνεῦμα Κυρίου   = 2736.

The total including τοῖς is 5622 which may be
Φῶς Κυρίου, ἡ ἐξουσία Ἰησοῦ Χριστοῦ.
$$2500 + 8 + 746 + 2368 = 5622.$$

The lesser total 5042 is not so clear.

And I also say unto thee that thou art Peter.
Κἀγὼ δέ σοι λέγω ὅτι σὺ εἶ Πέτρος.
$$824 + 8 + 280 + 838 + 380 + 600 + 15 + 755 = 3701.$$

Kephas the rock of the Church, the power to forgive
sins.
Κηφᾶς ἡ Πέτρα ἐκκλησίας, ἡ ἐξουσία ἀφιέναι ἁμαρτίας.
$$729 + 8 + 486 + 494 + 8 + 746 + 577 + 653$$
$$= 3701.$$

Note here that ἡ πέτρα ἐκκλησίας has the number
988 or Θησαυρός, Treasure, with an allusion to the
keys.   There is probably more on 3701.

"And upon this rock I will build my Church."

Καὶ ἐπὶ ταύτῃ   τῇ πέτρᾳ οἰκοδομήσω μου   τὴν
31 +95 +1009 +308 +486   +1292 +510 +358
ἐκκλησίαν.
+344   =4433.

Peter, the living Church of Jesus Christ.

Πέτρος, ἡ ἐκκλησία ζῶσα Ἰησοῦ Χριστοῦ   =4433.
Πέτρος, τὸ πανδοχεῖον Ἰησοῦ Χριστοῦ   =4433.
Πέτρος, μυστήριον, Φῶς Κυρίου   =4433.
Πέτρος, ἐξουσία τοῦ Θεοῦ σωτῆρος   =4433.

And gates of hell shall not prevail against it.

Καὶ πύλαι ᾅδου   οὐ κατισχύσουσιν αὐτῆς.
31 +521+475+470   +2461   +909   =4867.

Power of the Lord : The keys of hell and of death.

Δύναμις Κυρίου · αἱ κλεῖδες τοῦ θανάτου καὶ   τοῦ
705   +1000 +11 +274 +770 +831 +31+ 770
ᾅδου.
+475   =4867.

Τὸ φῶς μυστήριον πεντέρημα ἀφιέναι ἁμαρτίας.
1870   +1767   +1230   =4867.

Κηφᾶς τοῦ Κυρίου Ἰησοῦ Χριστοῦ   =4867.

[Καὶ] Δώσω σοὶ τὰς κλεῖς τῆς Βασιλείας τῶν
1804 +280 +501 +265 +508   +459 +1150
οὐρανῶν.
+1671 =6438 = 37 × 174.

[Καὶ] is omitted by the Revisers, who read κλεῖς and
not κλείδας.

This large multiple of 37 will have an indefinitely
large gematria, as will be readily understood.

We must be content to give a single example:—

Ἰησοῦς ὁ Χριστὸς   2438
Φῶς Κυρίου κατὰ μυστήριον   4000
                            ————
                            6438.

And whatsoever thou shalt bind on earth shall be
bound in heaven.

Καὶ ὃ ἐὰν δήσῃς ἐπὶ τῆς γῆς ἔσται δεδεμένον
31 +70 +56 +420+95+ 508 +211+516   +233
ἐν τοῖς ουρανοῖς.
+55+580 +901   = 3676.

Light of power to forgive sins.

Φῶς ἐξουσίας ἀφίεναι ἁμαρτίας.
1500 +946 +577 +653   = 3676.

Grace of God to forgive transgressions.

Χάρις Θεοῦ ἀφίεναι παραπτώματα.
911+484 +577 +1704   = 3676,
and conversely there is power to retain sins.

And whatsoever thou shalt loose on earth shall be
loosed in heaven.

Καὶ ὃ ἐὰν λύσῃς επὶ τῆς γῆς ἔσται λελυμένον ἐν τοῖς
οὐρανοῖς   = 4531.

Πέτρος+Ἰησοῦς Χριστὸς Σωτήρ.
755   +2368   +1408   = 4531.

Such is an outline, probably very meagre, of the
mysteries of this vitally important passage of Scripture.

THE TRANSFIGURATION.

In the summer of the year preceding our Lord's
Passion and Resurrection He seems to have gone
northward with His disciples; first to Caesarea Philippi
where, according to the Synoptic Gospels, He received
and accepted St. Peter's confession that He was the
Christ, and spoke of the Rock on which His Church
was to be built, but charged the disciples not to tell
anyone that He was the Christ. Thence proceeding
still northward He reached in about a week a very
high mountain, certainly Hermon and not Tabor, for

Tabor was a Roman camp. Only the three, St. Peter, St. James and St. John go with Him. It would seem almost like a holiday for quiet and refreshment, and is well placed in our Calendar in early August, and will shortly receive further recognition. The Lord had told His disciples what was to happen to Him and they had not understood. It was a turning point in His Ministry, and one reason for the retirement was prayer. And while He was praying there came a vision, or more than a vision. The form of His countenance was changed, He was transfigured and His clothes shone white with light. Also two appeared with Him who were recognised as Moses and Elijah, and these spoke of His "Exodus" at Jerusalem shortly to be accomplished by Him. But St. Luke alone mentions the subject of their speech.

Now in St. Luke's order of the Temptations in the Wilderness the Devil's challenge to do a miracle comes last, with the answer "Thou shalt not tempt the Lord thy God." This temptation had assailed both Moses and Elijah, the one at Massah and the other on Carmel. Each had failed to resist it, each had been suspended from his work and ordered to appoint a successor. Each had so passed from earth as to leave no known sepulchre, and the Assumption of Moses was as fully believed as that of Elijah. And these it was that spoke to the Lord, in the hearing of His disciples of His coming victory over His last temptation which came so fiercely on Him before Caiaphas, before Herod and on the Cross. He was to resist it and die. But as Moses and Elijah departed St. Peter made a speech, not knowing what he said, or at anyrate not its meaning. Yet it is put on record by all three Evangelists and its study is likely to be highly instructive. After the vocative Rabbi, Master, or Lord, St. Peter said :—

Κάλον ἐστιν ἡμᾶς ὧδε εἶναι.

171 + 565 + 249 + 809 + 76   = 1870

which is τὸ φῶς, and also τὸ ὄρος Σιών each being 1870.

"It is good for us to be here." They had entered the higher transcendental regions of space or The Light, where is the inheritance of the Saints (Col. I, 12, κληρονομία ἁγίων = 1263 = γνῶσις) or at least were very near it.

"Let us make here three tabernacles."

Καὶ ποιήσωμεν σκηνὰς τρεῖς.

31 + 1263 + 479 + 615   = 2388,

which is Πύλη φωτός or Ἰησοῦς + φῶς or Ἡ Θύρα φωτός as though they stood at the door of it and wished to stay at least near it. The rest of this sentence is:—

"One for Thee, one for Moses, and one for Elias."

Σοὶ μίαν καὶ Μωσῇ μίαν καὶ Ἠλίᾳ μίαν.

280 + 101 + 31 + 1048 + 101 + 31 + 49 + 101   = 1742.

On this number the interpretations may be

Τρία πρόσωπα	= 1742.
Three Aspects or Persons.	
Τὸ μὴ ὄν · τόπος Θεοῦ	= 1742.
That which Is Not : the Place of God.	
Εὕρημα θησαυροῦ	= 1742.
The Finding of the Treasure.	
Ἀλήθεια σωτῆρος	= 1742.
Θησαυρός, ἡ ἐξουσία	= 1742.

The actual text of the passage requires some critical attention.

The first clause is identical in all the three accounts.

The second is the reading in St. Mark and St. Luke, but St. Matthew has a variant which is this: St. Peter says,

Εἰ θέλεις ποιήσω ὧδε σκηνάς τρεῖς.

15 + 259 + 1168 + 809 + 479 + 615   = 3345.

"If Thou wilt I will make here three tabernacles,"
and

Δύναμις τοῦ φωτός.

705 + 770 + 1870   = 3345·

The third is identical in all three accounts except for
the order of the words which, for present purposes,
is immaterial. But there arises the question of the
spelling and declension of the name Moses, and to
a less degree Elias. This is a matter in which the
critic is entirely at the mercy of the MS. writers. And
we select Μωσῇ from St. Matthew, where the Revisers
read it, as in other places but not in all, and decline it
in the first declension, and proceed on that hypothesis.
The numbers then will be

$$1870$$
$$2388$$
$$1742$$
$$\overline{}$$
$$6000 = 4 \times 1500, \text{ a quadruple } φῶς,$$

and also

Ἡ μεταμόρφωσις, Ἐπίγνωσις Ἰησοῦ Χριστοῦ.

8   + 2266   + 1358   + 2368   = 6000

and if the first two alone are added the same idea is
kept, for 1870 + 2388   = 4258,
and

Ἡ μεταμόρφωσις φῶς Θεοῦ.

8   + 2266   + 1500 + 484   = 4258.

This number is also

Φῶς Κυρίου γεωμετρία ἐκκλησίας.

1500 + 1000   + 1264   + 494   = 4258,

and 0·2500 (φῶς Κυρίου) are the digits of the tesseract
$\left(\dfrac{\sqrt{2}}{2}\right)^{4}$ or the tesseract on $\left(\dfrac{\sqrt{2}}{2}\right)^{3}$ which contains the
tetrahedron whose edge is 1·000 and whose content
is ·1178.

It is also

Φῶς· Θησαυρὸς τοῦ Κυρίου.

1500 +988 +770+1000   =4258

and θησαυρὸς is a great gnostic symbol, standing apparently for π^2 or $(\sqrt{\pi})^4$.

This value is otherwise expressed in the mystical number 9879 (*i.e.* 9880−1), being that of the Psephos or stone given by our Lord to His disciples in the Bruce Codex The fourth root of this number (9·879) is 1·773 nearly, which is one-half of 3·546 (πίστεις ὡς κόκκος σινάπεως or Μυστήριον Ἰησοῦ Χριστοῦ).

But here a word of caution is needed. It is possible that the gnostic author of the Bruce Codex confused $(7 \times \sqrt{2})$ with π^2. For $7 \times \sqrt{2} = 9·9$ almost exactly. But 9·9 is not the same as 9·88 a figure already in excess of π^2, which is nearer 9·87 or 9·869. There is probably that difference between the Seven Amens and the Seven Voices which the Pistis Sophia actually regards as synonymous.

The next mystery seems to be

Νεφέλη φωτεινή or bright cloud.

598 + 1673   = 2271,

which is the gnosis (or the Cross) of the Lord :—

Ἡ γνῶσις (or σταυρὸς) Κυρίου.

1271   1271 + 1000   = 2271,

out of which comes the voice which said

Οὗτος ἐστιν ὁ Υἱὸς μου ὁ ἀγαπητὸς.

1040+565+70+680+510+70 +663   = 3598.

Αὐτοῦ ἀκούετε.

1171 +801   = 1972.

"This is My beloved Son : hear Him."

St. Matthew inserts ἐν ᾧ εὐδόκησα = 1563. In St. Luke an alternative reading ἐκλελεγμένος is preferred by the Revisers. But this would mean "chosen" or even "selected," a wholly inapplicable word for 'the Only begotten Son of God.' Its gematria is 463 instead of the 663 of ἀγαπητός. And ἐν ᾧ εὐδόκησα belongs to the voice at the Baptism.

And for interpretations :—

Ἰησοῦς Χριστὸς ἐξουσία Θεοῦ	= 3598.
Ἡ γνῶσις, ὁ Σωτὴρ · Ἡ μονὰς ἐν τρίαδι	= 3598.
Ἰησοῦς Θεὸς Κύριος	= 1972.

By addition, the whole passage $3598 + 1972 = 5570$, which is $1870 \, (τὸ \, φῶς) + 3700$, again a mystical number of Jesus Christ.

The voice at the Baptism would seem to be

Σὺ   εἶ   ὁ   Υἱός   μου   ὁ   ἀγαπητὸς,   ἐν   σοὶ
600 + 15 + 70 +680+510 + 70   +663 + 55 +280

εὐδόκησα.
$\qquad$ +708 $\qquad\qquad\qquad\qquad$ = 3651.

For this

Ὁ Λόγος Κυρίου Σωτὴρ κόσμου	= 3651.
Ὄνομα σωτηρίας Κυρίου Α. Ω.	= 3651.

But the various readings including the question of the augment on εὐδόκησα make the problem very difficult.

It seems clear that all the problems with which the "Lower criticism" can deal, have not been solved, and that it still is a proper subject for reverent and hopeful study.

The Transfiguration affords one instance out of many in which these strange correspondences of numbers occur in passages intended to be regarded as important, and in the most important portions of those passages. If any one can conceive of such correspondences existing in such a volume as the New Testament by mere accident, he must give up all belief in inspiration. God and His servants the Apostles must have known of their existence. God by immediate knowledge, man by some process of conscious or unconscious thought receiving impulses from the æon that is so near and yet so far. Further than this it is not easy even to attempt explanation. But the Light was manifested and Pistis Sophia must needs aspire to it, and if she fall into Chaos, she can repent and the Lord will save her.

THE ANNUNCIATION OF THE VIRGIN.
St. Luke i, 28.

"Hail, thou that art highly favoured, the Lord is with thee."

Χαῖρε	716
κεχαριτωμένη	1939
	——2655
Ὁ	70
Κύριος	800
μετὰ	346
σοῦ	670
	——1886
	4541

for which we may read:—

"Mary, a Virgin: the Mother of the Lord God."

Μαριὰμ· Παρθένος, ἡ μήτηρ Θεοῦ Κυρίου.

192   +515 +8 +456+484 +1000   =2655.

Εὔα+Χριστός.

406 +1480   =1886.

Κτίσις Πνεύματος   =1886.

Πνεῦμα+Ἄνθρωπος.

576   +1310   =1886,

and for the total

"The Fulness of Jesus Christ + The Mother of God."

Τὸ πλήρωμα Ἰησοῦ Χριστοῦ+Θεότοκος.

370 +1059   +2368   +744   =4541.

Τὸ μυστήριον κεκρυμμένον Σωτῆρος+Παρθένος =4541.

Κύριος Ἰησοῦς Χριστὸς Λόγος Κυρίου   =4541.

[Εὐλογημένη σὺ   ἐν γυναιξίν] omitted by Revisers.

619 +600+55 +584   =1858.

Μυστήριον+Υἱὸς.

1178 +680   =1858.

Μὴ φοβοῦ Μαριάμ. "Fear not, Mary" (v. 30).
48 + 1042 + 192   = 1282.
  Ἐξουσία, Γαβριὴλ ὁ ἄγγελος.
  746   + 154+70 +312   = 1282.
"For thou hast found favour with God."
Εὗρες γὰρ χάριν παρὰ τῷ Θεῷ.
710+ 104+761 + 182+ 1100+814   = 3671.

A Son of Grace: the Holy Spirit of the Lord.
  Ὑιὸς χαρίτος · Πνεῦμα ἅγιον Κυρίου.
  680 + 1281 + 576 + 134 + 1000   = 3671.
  Ἡ γνῶσις τοῦ ἁγίου Πνεύματος   = 3671.

Καὶ ἰδού, συλλήψῃ ἐν γάστρι.
31+484 + 1376+ 55 +614   = 2560.
  Ἰησοῦς Χριστὸς + Μαριάμ.
  2368 + 192   = 2560.

  Ἰησοῦς + Μαριάμ.
  888 + 192 = 1080 = Τὸ ἅγιον Πνεῦμα.

Χριστὸς,   1480
Τὸ ἅγιον Πνεῦμα,   1080
    ⎯⎯⎯⎯
    2560   = 2560.

Compare "Go thy way, thy son liveth," p. 68.
  Πορεύου ὁ υἱὸς σου ζῇ   = 2560.

Καὶ τέξῃ υἱόν. "And bring forth a son" (v. 31).
31 + 373 + 530   = 934.
  "And shalt call his name Jesus."
Καὶ καλέσεις τὸ ὄνομα αὐτοῦ Ἰησοῦν.
31 + 471 + 370 + 231 + 1171 + 738   = 3012.
          ⎯⎯⎯⎯
          3946.
Τὸ ἅγιον πνεῦμα, μυστήριον Κυρίου Ἰησοῦ.
1080 + 1178 + 1688   = 3946.

Διαθήκη Κυρίου, Ἰησοῦς ὁ υἱὸς ἐκ τῆς παρθένου.
60 + 1000 + 888+70+680+25+508 +715
          = 3946.

Μυστήριον Ἰησοῦς Ὕψιστος.
　1178　　+888　+1880　　　　　　　　　=3946.

"He shall be great."
Οὗτος ἔσται μέγας.
　1040 +516+249　　　　　　　　　　=1805.

"And shall be called the Son of the Highest."
Καὶ υἱὸς ὑψίστου κληθήσεται.
　31+680 +2080　　　+591　　　　　　=3382.
　　　　　　　　　　　　　　　　　　　　　―――
　　　　　　　　　　　　　　　　　　　5187.

Κύριος Μεσσίας Ἰσραήλ.
　800　　+656　+349　　　　　　　　　=1805.

Η ἀληθὴς διαθήκη Ἰακώβ.
　8 +256　　+60 +833　　　　　　　　=1805.

Μεσσίας · Ῥῆμα Κυρίου　　　　　　　=1805.

Ἰησοῦς ὁ Υἱὸς μονογενὴς ἐκ τῆς παρθένου　=3382.

Χριστὸς Μεσσίας ὁ Υἱὸς μονογενής　　=3382.

Θεὸς Ἰησοῦς Μονογενὴς τοῦ Πατρὸς ὁ Υἱὸς ἐκ τῆς
284 +888　　　+496+770 +751+70+680+25+508
　　　παρθένου.
　　　+715　　　　　　　　　　　　=5187.

"And the Lord God shall give unto him the throne
　　　of his father David."
Καὶ δώσει αὐτῷ Κύριος ὁ Θεὸς τὸν θρόνον Δαβὶδ
31 +1019+1501 +800 +70 +284+420 +349 +21
　　　τοῦ πατρὸς αὐτοῦ.
　　　+770 +751+1171　　　　　　　=7187.

Ἰησοῦς Χριστὸς　　　　=2368.

Υἱὸς ὑψίστου
680 +2080　　　　　　=2760.

Ὁ Βασιλεὺς αἰώνιος
70 +848　+1141　　　　=2059.
　　　　　　　　　　　　―――
　　　　　　　　　　　　　=7187.

(Πλήρωμα Κυρίου=2059.)

"And he shall reign over the house of Jacob for ever."

Καὶ βασιλεύσει ἐπὶ τὸν οἶκον 'Ιακὼβ εἰς τοὺς αἰῶνας.

31   +863   +95+420+220   +833+215+970 +1062
                                                    =4709.

'Ο Σταυρὸς Κυρίου 'Ιησοῦ Χριστοῦ.

70 +1271 +1000   +2368   =4709.

"And of his Kingdom there shall be no end."

Καὶ τῆς βασιλείας αὐτοῦ οὐκ ἔσται τέλος.

31+508   +459 +1171+490 +516 +605   =3780.

'Ιησοῦς ὁ Μεσσίας ὁ μέλλων αἰώνιος.

888+70 +656+70 +955 +1141   =3780.

Ζωὴ αἰώνιος

815+1141   =1956.

'Ο αἰὼν ὁ μέλλων.

70+861+70+955   =1956.

'Ιησοῦς+Μαριὰμ Θεοτόκος.

888   +192   +744 +1956   =3780.
⎵‾‾‾‾‾‾‾‾‾‾‾⎵
   1080

Then follows the Blessed Virgin's question in which we look for nothing but its plain meaning and after which the angel continues :—

I. 35.

"The Holy Ghost shall come upon thee."

Πνεῦμα ῞Αγιον ἐπελεύσεται ἐπὶ σέ.

576 +134   +1041 +95+205   =2051

Παρθενος Μήτηρ+Τὸ ῞Αγιον Πνεῦμα.

515   +456   +1080   =2051.

Λόγος Σωτῆρος.

373 +1678   =2051.

Παρθενος+῾Η γεωμετρία 'Αληθείας.

515   +1536   =2051.

"And the power of the Highest shall overshadow
        thee."

Καὶ δύναμις Ὑψίστου ἐπισκιάσει σοι.

31   +705   +2080   +541 +280   = 3637.

Δύναμις τοῦ Θεοῦ Σωτῆρος.
  705+770+484 +1678   = 3637.

Κύριος Σωτήρ, τὸ πλήρωμα.
  800 +1408+370 +1059   = 3637.

Κύριος Ἰησοῦς+καταπέτασμα Κυρίου.
  800   +888   +949   +1000   = 3637.

"Therefore also the holy thing which is to be born,
shall be called the Son of God."

Διὸ καὶ τὸ γεννώμενον ἅγιον κληθήσεται Υἱὸς Θεοῦ.
84+31+370 +1123   +134   +591   +680 +484
                                                    = 3497.

Ἐκ σοῦ is omitted by the Revisers.

Ὁ Λόγος ἐκ Πατρὸς, ὁ Κύριος Σωτήρ.
70 +373 +25 +751+70 +800 +1408   = 3497.

Ὁ Λόγος κατὰ μυστήριον, Μεσσίας ἡμῶν.
70 +373+322   +1178   +656 +898   = 3497.

Ὁ Ἀμνὸς Θεοῦ, Ἰησοῦς ὁ Υἱὸς Θεοτόκου.
70 +361 +484   +888+70+680   +944   = 3497.

Ἰησοῦς ὁ μονογενὴς Θεοτόκου, Μεσσίας ὁ Λόγος.
888+70 +496   +944   +656+70+373 = 3497.

I. 36.

"And, behold, thy cousin Elizabeth."

Καὶ ἰδού, Ἐλισάβετ ἡ συγγενίς σου.
31+484   +553 +8 +871+670   = 2617.

          Ἡλίας   249
          Ἰησοῦς Χριστὸς   · 2368
                                 ————
                                 2617.

"She hath also conceived a son in her old age."

Καὶ αὐτὴ συνείληφεν υἱὸν ἐν τῇ γήρᾳ αὐτῆς.
31+709 +1258 +300+55+308+112+909   = 3912.

Ἰωάννης πρόδρομος 1853
Πλήρωμα Κυρίου 2059
————=3912.

Ἰωάννης Ζαχαρίου ὁ Πρόδρομος 3112
Κύριος 800
————=3912.

1119 +1189+70 +734 +800 =3912.'
800 may also be Θεοῦ ἀληθὴς διαθήκη.

Καὶ οὗτος μὴν ἕκτος ἐστὶν αὐτῇ τῇ καλουμένῃ στείρᾳ.
31+1040+98 +595+565+709+308 +624 +616
=4586.

Ἐλισάβετ μήτηρ, θυγατὴρ Ἀαρών.
553 +456 +821 +952 =2782
Ὁ Πρόδρομος Κυρίου.
70 +734 +1000 =1804
————=4586.

It is also
Ἐλισάβετ ἡ συγγενίς σου 2102
Ὁ Πρόδρομος Χριστοῦ 2484
————=4586.

Ὅτι οὐκ ἀδυνατήσει παρὰ τοῦ Θεοῦ πᾶν ῥῆμα.
380+490 +979 +182+770+484+131+149
=3565.

Τὸ μυστήριον Κυρίου Ἐλισάβετ ἡ μήτηρ.
370 +1178 +1000 +553 +8 +456 =3565.
Μυστήριον Χριστοῦ Μαριὰμ Παρθένος.
1178 +1680 +192 +515 =3565.
Ἰωάννης ὁ προφήτης Παραμύθιον Ἰσραήλ.
1119+70 +1266 +761 +349 =3565.

I. 38.

"Behold the handmaid of the Lord."
Ἰδού, ἡ δούλη Κυρίου.
484+8 +512 +1000 =2004.

Τὸ μυστήριον+μήτηρ.
1548 +456 =2004.

"Be it unto me according to thy Word."

Γένοιτό μοι κατὰ τὸ ῥῆμά σου.
508 + 120 + 322 + 370 + 149 + 670   = 2139.

Μαριὰμ ἡ Παρθένος Θεότοκος + Υἱός.
192 + 8   + 515   + 744 + 680   = 2139.

Adding both portions 2004 + 2139 = 4143.

Τὸ μυστήριον, Μαριὰμ Παρθένος Θεότοκος Μήτηρ
370   + 1178   + 192   + 515   + 744   + 456
       Ἰησοῦ.
       + 688   = 4143.

This is also 3700 + 443 = 4143.

Ὁ Λόγος   Θεομήτωρ.
70 + 373   + 2368   + 1332   = 4143.
‾‾‾‾‾‾
443

and probably much more.

PREFACE TO THE 37 SERIES.

In an appendix to our "Preliminary Investigation" we exhibited the earlier indications that led us to believe that there was a systematic tendency observable in Christian titles and phrases to be multiples of 37 when the numeral values of the letters composing them were added together.

According to the law of chances only some three per cent. should appear. Anything more would point to design of some sort. That is, if it were not by accident it must be of purpose, and if so the purpose would naturally be of an important sort. As the work continued the list grew and its present state is now published. It will be seen that when once the multiples are high enough to allow of the use of the letters that signify the hundreds (ρ to ω) the Christian gematria becomes very large and significant.

Even from the commencement the phenomenon is apparent, but when such numbers as 2368, ᾽Ιησοῦς Χριστὸς (already published) and 2960, Υἱὸς τοῦ ἀνθρώπου provide such lists as are shown, and others scarcely less important results, the inference becomes irresistible that there is something here which cannot be regarded as accidental.

Sporadically there will be found other numbers not multiples of 37 which yield good gematria. This must necessarily be the case. But no other series of multiples shows anything like the system and symmetry that these multiples of 37 show. Experiments have been

tried on other numbers but have failed. The sporadic
numbers do not usually fall into arithmetical sequence.
They have their meanings and can probably be grouped
geometrically, though this is not yet in all cases
apparent.

But what is apparent is that the multiples of this
one number, 37, are connectible with Christian theological nomenclature to the amazing extent here shown.
They centre round the Divine Name and title of Jesus
Christ and His own title Son of Man. It has been
already shown that Θεότης, Godhead, added to Ἰησοῦς
give the number of Χριστὸς and all three together make
up Υἱὸς τοῦ ἀνθρώπου. To anyone who believes in
inspiration, the pre-knowledge of God in this will be
plain. And also in all that is now put in evidence,
human error in detail alone excepted. We, the scribes
of it, set it forth as we find it. Of our own power we
could not have made it. We only find it because it
exists. Here and there we may be in error in addition
or in copying, but such errors can be dealt with by
the simple process of erasure. The rest stands good,
but on its own merits and not on ours. We no more
made what is in the New Testament than one of us
made Glastonbury or the other the flora and fauna of
an Atlantic island. We only found what we found, and
have published what we found and how we found it.

This list is an appeal to facts, an appeal from jarring
strife about words and opinions. It needs no ecclesias-
tical authority, it requires no defence. The one question
that may be asked is as to relevance, or relation to
other truth. And here the authors take courage and

incur risk. These things are relevant to the interpretation of what is called by St. Paul and others
"The Gnosis." It may also be relevant to what are
called "Tongues" or the interpretation of Tongues.
And "Tongues" may be of "divers kinds." These
are avowedly things that may be rendered useless
(καταργηθήσονται) or cease. But things corresponding
to those names, Gnosis and Glossai, did exist and had
their uses. And it is not impossible that they may
be revived.

With this challenge we leave the list as it stands in
Greek. Our English translations may be faulty, but
can easily be corrected by any who disagree. We
hardly dare to speculate on the origin of language
which can thus bear testimony to the Gospel it
preached. But Christians do believe that some very
wonderful gift was conferred at the great Day of
Pentecost, and we incline to think we may not be
far wrong in believing that this was part of that gift.
But we speak that we do know and testify to that
we have seen, and wait to see whether our witness
will be received.

A Select List of Divine Names and Titles built upon the Metacube of Thirty-seven.

------

37   'Η θίβη.
= 37 × 1   The Ark of Bulrushes.   (Exodus ii. 3.)
         Cp. 370, οἶκος as a "spiritual House" (1 Pet. ii. 24).

*

74   Αἱ διαθῆκαι.
= 37 × 2   The Covenants.   (Ep. Rom. ix.)
         Cp. 740, αἷμα Ἰησοῦ.

111   Οἰκία.
= 37 × 3   The Fleshly Tabernacle or bodily abode of the
         Soul (2 Cor. v. 1).
         Cp. 1110 τόπος νόος.   ὁ μίκρος κόσμος.

148   'Η καθέδρα.
= 37 × 4   The Seat of Moses (Matt. xxiii. 2).
         Cp. 1480, θρόνος σοφίας.

185   'Ο 'Ραββί.
= 37 × 5   The Master.   Title of Christ.
         Cp. 1850, ἄνθρωπος διδάσκαλος.

222
= 37 × 6

259   Βασιλεία.
= 37 × 7   Kingdom.   Title of Christ.
         Εἱμαρμένη. (σφαῖρα.) (Pist. Soph.)
         Οἱ θέμελιοι.   The Foundations.
              Cp. 2590, ἡ σφαῖρα τοῦ Κυρίου.
                        τά πάντα καὶ ἐν πᾶσι Χριστός.
                        τόπος φωτός.

296   Κεράμιον.
= 37 × 8   Water-pitcher (Mark xiv. 13; Luke xxii. 10).
         The Cube of 2 is involved here as a geometrical
              principle: *cp.* 2960, ἡ γεωμετρία Κυρίου
              Ἰησοῦ, etc.

333   Ἡ ἐλπίς.
= 37 × 9   Hope. Title of Christ (Col. i. 27 ; 1 Tim. i. 1).
         Cp. 3330, ὁ Κύριος Σωτήρ. ἡ ἐλπὶς τῆς γῆς.
         Οἰκοδόμημα. A dwelling.

370   Οἶκος.
= 37 × 10   A spiritual House (1 Pet. ii. 24).
         (A figure of the regenerate, built as living
              stones into a spiritual temple.)

407   Ἡ κληρονομία.
= 37 × 11   The Inheritance. Type of Christ.

444   Σὰρξ καὶ αἷμα.
= 37 × 12   Flesh and Blood. (Symbol of the human
              nature of Jesus.)
         Ὁ ἄγρος. The field.

481   Ἡ γένεσις.
= 37 × 13   The Beginning. (Christ is also ἀλφά and
              ἀρχή and πρῶτος.)
         Ἡ ἐπισκοπή.
              The Lord's Visitation. (1 Pet. ii. 12.)

518   Ἡ θύρα.
= 37 × 14   The Door. Type of Christ.
              Cp. John x. 9. ἡ θύρα τῶν προβάτων = 3071.
         Ὁ λόγος ἐν ἰδέᾳ.
              Athenagoras' definition of Christ as the
                   second person of the Trinity.
         Οἴκησις. A dwelling. *Cp.* 111, 370, 333.

555   Διάκρισις.
= 37 × 15   Spiritual Discernment.   (Ep. Heb. v. 14.)

592   Θεότης, Godhead   ⎫   ⎧Πατήρ, Father.
= 37 × 16   Ἁγιότης, Holiness   ⎬ = 1776 = ⎨Ὑιός, Son.
           Ἀγαθότης, Goodness   ⎭   ⎩καὶ Πνεῦμα and Spirit.

   Ἡ ἐκκλησία ἡ πᾶσα.
   The whole Church.

629   Ἀληθὴς λόγος.
= 37 × 17   Very Word.   (See Origen *v.* Celsus.)

666   Ὁ σπαρείς.
= 37 × 18   The Seed-corn.

   Ὁ σπείρας.
   The Sower of Tares.   (The number of the
    Beast of the Apocalypse.)

   Λόγος ἀγάπης.
   Word of Love.

703   Ὁ θεὸς Ἰσραήλ.
= 37 × 19   The God of Israel.

   Ὁ ἅγιος Ἰσραήλ.
   The Holy One of Israel (Title of Christ).

   Θεὸς Δαυίδ.
   God of David.

740   Αἷμα Ἰησοῦ.
= 37 × 20   Blood of Jesus.

   Ἁγίασμα θεοῦ.
   The Consecrated Wafer (Eccl.)
   Holiness (Psa. xcii. 5).

777   Τὰ ἔνοντα.
= 37 × 21   The Inward Things (Luke xi. 41).

   Οἱ καλοὶ μαργαρίται.
   The goodly Pearls.

   Οἱ κλητοὶ βασιλείᾳ.
   Those called to the Kingdom.

814 ʽΟ λόγος (ζῶν καὶ) ἐνεργής.
= 37 × 22   The Powerful Word of God.

> See ὁ λόγος ζῶν καὶ ἐνεργής.   814 + 888 = 1702
> = Ἰησοῦς ὁ ἐνεργὴς λόγος.   (*Cp.* Ep. Heb.
> iv. 12.)

814 ʽΗ θεῖα σοφία.
= 37 × 22   The Divine Wisdom.

851 Ὕπαρξις.
= 37 × 23   Substance. Type of Christ. (Heb. x. 34.)

> Θεότης + Βασιλεία.

888 Ἰησοῦς.
= 37 × 24   Jesus. (Παρθένος 515 + Λόγος 373.)

> "For Jesus (Ἰησοῦς) is a Name arithmetically
> symbolical consisting of six letters, and is
> known by all those that belong to the
> Called." (Irenaeus. Haer. I. viii. 5. Har-
> vey, vol. I, p. 136. Also pp. 149 and 334.)
> (For other examples see list published in Part I.)

925 Πᾶσα ἐκκλησία Ἰσραήλ.
= 37 × 25   The whole Church of Israel.

> Ἐκκλησία ἐπὶ πέτραν.
> The Church upon a Rock.
>
> Διαθήκη εἰρήνης Θεοῦ.
> Covenant of the Peace of God.
>
> ʽΟ Νωέ.
> Noah. Type of the Regenerate.

962 Ὅρασις εἰρήνης.
= 37 × 26   Beatific Vision. Vision of Peace.

> IHVH-ShLM.
> Jehovah-Shalom = Jah is Peace.
> (Name of Gideon's Altar.)
>
> Τριὰς τελεία.
> Perfect Trinity. (Creed of Gregory.)

999   Εἷς Θεὸς ὁ Μνόος.
= 37 × 27   One God, the Only One.
    Ὁ ἀπόρρητος.
        The Ineffable One.
    Ἡ παραμυθία Ἰσραήλ.
        The Consolation of Israel.
    Παράκλησις Ἰσραήλ.
        The Consolation of Israel.

1036   Ἡ ἐξανάστασις.
= 37 × 28   The Resurrection.
    (Ἡ ἀνάστασις εἰμί.)
    Ἡ πᾶσα ἐξουσία.
        The "full Authority" committed to Christ.
    Ὁ θεὸς καὶ τὸ ἄρνιον.
        God and the Lamb (Rev. xxi).

1073   Ἡ ὅρασις Θεοῦ.
= 37 × 29   The Vision of God.
    Ὁ Θεὸς τῆς γῆς.
        The God of the Earth (Gen. xxiv. 3).
    Ἡ ἔποψις.
        The Mystic Vision.

1110   Τὰ πάντα καὶ ἐν πᾶσι.
= 37 × 30   All and In All (of Christ) (Coloss. iii. 11).
    Υἱὸς μόνος.
        Only Son. (Of Christ).
    Παραμύθιον Ἰσραήλ.
        Consolation of Israel.
    Ὁ σοφός.
        The Wise.

1147   Μάντευμά τι.
= 37 × 31   That Principle which is above the Human
        Intelligence (Plato).

Οὐσία ἄπειρος.
Infinite Essence or Being.
Παρθένος οὐρανία.
Heavenly Virgin (Type of spiritual Wisdom).

1184 Α · Ω · ’Αμὴν · Θεός.
= 37 × 32   First : Last : Amen : God.

    Εἷς κύριος · Ὁ ἀμήν.
       One Lord : the Amen.

    ’Αμὴν · Μόνος ἐκ μόνου.
       Amen : Only (God) of Only (God).

    Τελεστικὴ ἐπιπνοία.
       Sublime Inspiration (Plato).

    Ο κοσμόποιος Θεός.
       God the World-creating.

    ’Εν ἑτέρα μορφῇ.
       Jesus on the road to Emmaus.   (1184 × 2 = 2368.)
    (See also the Transfiguration.)

1221 Ὁ Θεὸς δι’ ὃν τὰ πάντα.
= 37 × 33   God for Whom are All Things (Heb. ii. 10).

    Θαυμαστός.
       Wonderful (Title of the Messiah).   (Isa. ix. 6.)

    Μεσσίας ἐστίν.
       He is Messiah.

1258 Ὁ λειτουργός.
= 37 × 34   The Minister (Type of Christ).   (Heb. ix. 15.)

    Ἡ σκηνὴ ἡ λειτουργική.
       The Tabernacle of the Ministry.

1295 ’Ακατάληπτος Θεός.
= 37 × 35   God Incomprehensible.

    Διαθήκη Θεοῦ Πατρός.
       Covenant of God the Father.

Οἱ παῖδες τοῦ Ἀβραάμ.
:   The Children of Abraham.

Οἴκημα πνεύματος.
:   Habitation of the Spirit.

Τὸ ῥῆμα ἐκ Πατρός.
:   The Word of the Father.

1332   Ἄλφα · Ω.
= 37 × 36   First : Last.   (Title of Christ.)

Ἀληθῶς Θεός.
:   Very God.

Σῶσον δή.
:   Hosannah!

Θεότης ἐκ παρθένου.
:   Godhead from a Virgin.

Ἰησοῦς · Σὰρξ καὶ αἷμα.
:   Jesus : Flesh and Blood.

1369   Θεὸς μόνος ἐκ μόνου.
= 37 × 37   God, the Only of the Only One.

Ὁ Θεὸς ζωῆς.
:   The God of Life.

Εἷς Θεὸς ὁ Κύριος.
:   One God, the Lord.

Ἡ μονὰς Κυρίου.
:   The Unity of God.

Οὐσία Ἰησοῦ.
:   Substance of Jesus.

Εἰκὼν Θεοῦ.
:   Image of God.

Ἔσοπτρον ἐκκλησίας.
:   Mirror of the Church.   (Εἴσοπτρον Θεοῦ.)

Υἱὸς καὶ κληρονόμος.
:   Son and Heir (Titles of Christ).   (Gal. iv. 7.)

1406 Ὁ υἱὸς · Μεσσίας.
= 37 × 38   The Son : Messiah.

Μορφὴ Ἰησοῦ.
Form of Jesus.

Ἀληθινὸν μυστήριον.
True Mystery.

Ἀρχαὶ ὀθόνης μεγάλης.
Corners of the Great Sheet (Vision of Peter)

1443 Ὁ λόγος Κυρίου.
= 37 × 39   The Word of the Lord.

Ὁ μέγας λόγος Πατρός.
The Great Word of the Father.

Ὑιὸς · Μεσίτης.
Son : Mediator.

Θεῖος λόγος ἐκ Πατρὸς.
Divine Word from the Father.

Η εἰρήνη τοῦ Θεοῦ.
The Peace of God.

Ἄρτος τῆς ἀληθείας.
Bread of Truth.

Ὁ ἄρτος ὁ ἀθάνατος.
The Bread Immortal.

Ὁ Μεσσίας · Ἡ ἀρχή.
The Messiah : The Beginning.

Ὁ Ἀμὴν · Θεὸς ἐκ Θεοῦ · Ἡ γένεσις.
The Amen : God of God : The Beginning.

1480 Χριστός (see collected list 2368).
= 37 × 40   Ὁ πανδοχεύς.
The Host. (Parable of the Good Samaritan.)

Ἡ ἁγιωσύνη.
The Holiness.

Ὑιὸς · Κύριος.
Son : Lord.

Θεῖον γεννητόν κόσμου.
> The "Divine Event" of the World (Plato).

Μάθησις σφαίρας.
> Doctrine of the Sphere.

Καινὴ φιλοσοφία.
> The New Philosophy.

Ἡ ἀνεωγμένη θυρὰ.
> The Open Door.

Λίθος τρισεπάπειρος.
> Stone of the Three "dimensions." (Compare Clem. Hom. xvii. 9.)

1517   Θεότης Μεσσιοῦ.
= 37 × 41   Godhead of the Messiah.

Ἡ ἀρχὴ · Κύριος.
> The Beginning : Lord.

Δύναμις καὶ σοφία.
> Power and Wisdom. (Types of Christ.)

Γένος τοῦ Δαυίδ.
> Race of David. (Type of Christ.)

Φωνὴ μέγαλη · Ἡ ἀλήθεια.
> A Great Voice : The Truth.

Ὁ πᾶς λόγος · Θεὸς ἐκ Θεοῦ.
> The All-Word : God of God.

Ἰησοῦς · Ἀληθὴς λόγος.
> Jesus : True Word.

Οἱ λόγοι τοῦ Θεοῦ.
> The Words of God.

Κατασκευασμένος.
> Prepared (for the Lord). (Luke i. 17.)

Πέτρος ὁ κύβος.
> Peter the Stone. (*cp*. Clem. Hom. xvii.)

1554   Θεότης θεοτήτος.
= 37 × 42   Godhead of Godhead.

Μόνος λόγος Πατρός.
> Only Word of the Father.

Ὁ λόγος καὶ τὸ Ἅγιον Πνεῦμα.
> The Word and the Holy Spirit.

Ἰησοῦς · Λόγος ἀγάπης.
> Jesus : Word of Love.

Μέγιστος Κύριος.
> Greatest Lord.

Μεσσίας ἡμῶν.
> Our Messiah.

Ἀνάστασις σαρκός.
> Resurrection of the Flesh.

Τὰ χαρίσματα.
> The Spiritual Gifts.

Κηφᾶς ὁ πέτρος.
> Cephas the Stone.

Ἐπιφανεία κύβου.
> Manifestation of the Cube or Surface.

Ἅλας κυβομορφον.
> Salt-Crystal.

Ἡ πᾶσα γεωμετρία.
> The All-Geometry.

1591 Πᾶς ἄνθρωπος.
= 37 × 43 All Humanity. (Col. i. 28.)

Ἄλφα · Πλήρωμα (πατρότης).
> First : Fulness (Fatherhood).

Τῷ πατρί.
> To the Father.

Αἰωνοτόκος.
> Father of the Aeon. (Synesius.)

Πνεῦμα ζωῆς.
> Spirit of Life.

Ἡ διαθήκη τῆς ζωῆς.
> The Covenant of Life.

1628 Κεφάλη γωνίας.
= 37 × 44 Head of the Corner. (Matt. xxi. 42.)

  Ὁ ἐξάγωνος λίθος.
   The Cube.

  Τὰ χρηστήρια.
   The Oracles.

  Ζωὴ ἐκ Πατρός.
   Life from the Father.

  Καρπὸς τῆς μήτρας.
   Fruit of the Womb. (Type of Christ.)

  Ἀναγέννησις ἐκ νέκρων.
   Resurrection from the Dead.

  Ἡ θυσία Κυρίου.
   The Lord's Sacrifice.

1665 Ἄλφα · Ὦμεγα · Θεός
= 37 × 45 First : Last : God.

  Ἁ καὶ Ω · ὁ Μεσίτης.
   First and Last : the Mediator.

  Ὁ Υἱὸς · ὁ Ἀμνὸς Θεοῦ.
   The Son : the Lamb of God.

  Ὁ μονογενὴς Λόγος · ὁ Μεσσίας.
   The Only-begotten Word : the Messiah.

  Ἔξω Κύριος.
   Transcendent Lord.

  Εἰρήνη Θεοῦ Κυρίου.
   Peace of God the Lord.

1702 Α καὶ Ω · ὁ Κύριος.
= 37 × 46 First and Last : the Lord.

  Τὸ Ἄλφα · Κύριος.
   The First : Lord.

  Ὦμεγα · ἡ μονὰς Θεοῦ.
   Last : the Unity of God.

Ζωὴ εἰς τὸ διήνεκες.
   Life Everlasting.

Εἰρήνη τοῦ πατρός.
   Peace of the Father.

Χαρὰ Κυρίου.
   Joy of the Lord.

Ἡ βασιλεία κατὰ Γνῶσιν.
   The Kingdom according to Knowledge.

1739   Υἱὸς · Πλήρωμα.
= 37 × 47   A Son : Fulness.

Ἰησοῦς · Ὑπάρξις.
   Jesus : True Substance.

Χριστὸς · Βασιλεία.
   Christ (the) Kingdom.

Ζῶν λόγος ἐκ Θεοῦ.
   Living Word from God.

Ἀνάστασις ἐκ Πατρός.
   Resurrection from the Father.

Ὁ Κύριος βοηθός μου.
   The Lord my Helper (Psalms).

Ὁ βοηθὸς ὁ μύστικος.
   The Mystic Helper.

1776   Θεότης ἐν ἑτέρᾳ μορφῇ.
= 37 × 48   Godhead in another Form (as of Jesus on the
         road to Emmaus).

Ἀποκάλυψις ἀληθείας.
   Revelation of Truth.

Πατὴρ Υἱὸς καὶ Πνεῦμα.
   Father, Son, and Holy Spirit.

Ἡ σωτηρία Ἰσραήλ.
   The Salvation of Israel (Title of Christ).

Ὁ Μεσσίας ἐκ νέκρων.
   The Messiah from the Dead.

'Ο Θεὸς + 'Η Μητὴρ + 'Ο Ἰησοῦς.
    God : the Mother, and Jesus.

'Η νίκη Χριστοῦ.
    The Victory of Christ.

Νίκη Κυρίου Ἰησοῦ.
    Victory of the Lord Jesus.

Ποταμὸς ζωῆς.
    River of Life (type of Christ).   (Rev. xxii.)

'Η ἀρχὴ · Πλήρωμα.
    The Beginning : Fulness.

Τὸ τέλος · Α · Ω.
    The End : First : Last.

'Η Κόρη τοῦ κόσμου.
    The Virgin of the World (Gnostic).

Τὸ ἀληθινόν μυστήριον.
    The True Mystery.

37 × 49 = 1813   Κύριος Σαβαώθ.
    Lord of Hosts.   (Septuagint.)

Ἀρχάγγελος κόσμου.
    Archangel of the World.   (N.B. Christ was
        called "archangel" by the early Fathers.)

Μιχαήλ · Λόγος Πατρός.
    Michael : Word of the Father.   (Suggested as
        a type of Christ.)

Ἐμμανουὴλ ὁ Υἱὸς Δαυίδ.
    Emmanuel, the Son of David.

'Ο Υἱὸς Δαυίδ κατὰ σάρκα.
    The Son of David after the Flesh.

Ἄλφα · Ὤμεγα · Ὁ ζῶν.
    First : Last : the Living One.

1850   Κύριος ἐκ νέκρων.
= 37 × 50   Lord from the Dead.

Ὄνομα σωτηρίας.
    Name of Salvation.

Βασιλεὺς τῆς ἐκκλησίας.
>King of the Church.

Τὰ δέξια τοῦ θρόνου.
>The Right Hand of the Throne.

Ὁ τόπος Σιών.
>Sion.

Ὁ γεωμέτρης ὁ μέγας.
>The Great Geometer.

Ἀρχὴ αἰώνιος.
>Eternal Beginning.

Ὁ Μεσσίας · Λόγος Πατρός.
>The Messiah : Word of the Father.

Λόγος σοφίας μονογενής.
>Word of Wisdom Only-begotten.

1887 Σωτήριον Ἰσραήλ.
= 37 × 51 Salvation of Israel (Title of the Messiah).

Τὸ γένος τοῦ Δαυίδ.
>The Race of David   (do.)

Λόγος Πατρός · Μεσίτης.
>Word of the Father : Mediator.

Τὸ ῥῆμα Κυρίου ἐνεργές.
>The Powerful Word of the Lord.

Ἰησοῦς ἡ παραμυθία Ἰσραήλ.
>Jesus the Consolation of Israel.

Εἰκὼν τῆς ἐκκλησίας.
>Image of the Church.

Κεφαλίτης λίθος ἐκκλησίας.
>Head Stone of the Church.

Ὁ τῆς μέγαλης βουλῆς ἀγγέλος. (This form is found in the Pistis Sophia. In the Septuagint it is μέγαλης βουλῆς ἀγγέλος.)

1924 Ἡ ἐπιφανεία τοῦ Θεοῦ.
= 37 × 52 The Manifestation of God

Ὁ κόσμος τοῦ Θεοῦ.
The Universe of God.

Λόγος Πατρός · Κύριος.
Word of the Father. Lord.

Ὁ λόγος Κυρίου · Ἡ γένεσις.
The Word of the Lord : the Beginning.

Ὁ οἰκὸς Θεοῦ Κυρίου.
Ὁ Υἱὸς · Λόγος · Α · Ω.
The Son : The Word First and Last.

Τὸ σημεῖον ἐκ πνεύματος.
The Sign from the Spirit

Τὸ ἅλας κυβόμορφον.
Salt Crystal.

Τὸ καλὸν σημεῖον Κυρίου.
The Good Sign of the Lord.

Ἡ οὐσία Θεοῦ Πατρός.
The Substance of God the Father.

Ὁ λόγος τῆς δικαιοσύνης.
The Word of Righteousness.

1961
= 37 × 53
Τὸ Ἄλφα · Πατρότης (or Πλήρωμα).
The First : Fatherhood, etc.

Ἀ καὶ Ω · Ὁ μέγας παράκλητος.
First and Last : great Paraclete.

Ἀ καὶ Ω · Ἡ προσφορά.
First and Last : the Offering.

Ἰσχυρά παράκλησις.
Strong Consolation (Heb. vi. 18).

Πλήρωμα χαρᾶς.
Fulness of Joy.

Ὁ Μεσσίας Θεοῦ Πατρός.
The Messiah of God the Father.

Πνεῦμα καὶ λόγος σοφίας.
Spirit and Word of Wisdom

Ὁ λίθος τῆς γωνίας.
The Corner-Stone.

Υἱὸς χάριτος.
Son of Grace.

Χριστὸς ἡ γένεσις.
Christ the Beginning.

1998   Ὁ Υἱὸς ἐκ τῆς Παρθένου.
= 37 × 54   The Son (born) of the Virgin.

Υἱὸς · Κεφάλη γυναικός.
Son : Head of the Woman.

Υἱὸς · Ἀλήθεια τοῦ Θεοῦ.
A Son : Truth of God.

Ἰησοῦς υἱός μόνος.
Jesus, the Only Son.

Ὁ υἱὸς ἀληθινὸς · Ὁ Κύριος.
The True Son : the Lord.

Ὁ μονογενὴς λόγος · Πλήρωμα.
The Only-begotten Word : Fulness.

Ὁ μονογενὴς · Μεσσίας ἐκ Πατρός.
Ὁ Χριστὸς ὁ ἀληθινός.
The True Anointed One.

Ἐνεργὴς λόγος τοῦ Θεοῦ.
Powerful Word of God.

Μεσίτης Θεοῦ Πατρός.
Mediator of God the Father.

Θεότης ἐν σώματι.
Godhead in the Flesh.

Ποιητὴς ἀοράτων.
Maker of the Invisible (Creeds).

Ζῶν Θεὸς · Λόγος Θεοῦ.
Living God : Word of God.

Λόγος Θεοῦ αἰώνιος.
Eternal Word of God.

Ἡ ἀρχὴ · Ὁ Θεὸς ὁ ζῶν.
The Beginning : the Living God.

Ἡ ἀρχὴ πάντων.
The Beginning of All Things.

Ὁ ʾΗν · Τὸ φῶς.
He Who Was : the Light.

Ἡ μεγάλη σωτηρία Θεοῦ.
The Great Salvation of God.

Α · Ω · ʽΗ δύναμις Θεοῦ.
First : Last : the Power of God.

ʾΑλφα · Ω · Λόγος ἀγάπης.
First : Last : Word of Love.

Τὸ ἄλφα · Ὁ Θεὸς ἀόρατος.
The First : the Unseen God.

Τὸ ὤμεγα · Τέλειος ἀνήρ.
The Last : Perfect Man.

2035   Τεῖχος πυρός.
=37×55   Wall of Fire. (Type of the Messiah, Zech. ii.)

Λόγος Θεοῦ · Μυστήριον·
Word of God : Mystery.

Κύριος · Καταβάσιον πῦρ.
The Lord a descending Fire.

Χριστὸς ἐν ὑμῖν.
Christ in you.

Ζῶν Κύριος ἀληθινός.
Living True Lord.

Εὐαγγέλιον τοῦ Ἰησοῦ.
Gospel of Jesus.

Σοφία τοῦ Θεοῦ.
Wisdom of God.

Ὁ Ναξωραῖος · Ὁ Μεσσίας.
The Nazarene : the Messiah.

Ὁ Υἱὸς τῆς ἀγάπης Θεοῦ.
The Son of God's Love.

ʽΗ δικαιοσύνη τοῦ Θεοῦ.
The Righteousness of God.

Εἰσηκούσθη ἡ δέησίς σου.
"Thy prayer is heard" (Luke i. 13).

2072 ʽΗ ἐκκλησία τοῦ Κυρίου.
= 37 × 56 The Church of the Lord.

ʽΗ γνῶσις · Α · Ω.
The Gnosis : First : Last.

Τὸ ἄλφα · Τὸ Ω.
The First : The Last

Χριστὸς θεότης.
Christ the Godhead.

Κύριος μονογενὴς ἐκ Πατρός.
Lord Only-begotten of the Father.

Γεωμετρικὴ σοφία.
Geometrical Wisdom.

ʽΟ Ναζωραῖος · Μεσίτης.
The Nazarene : Mediator.

2109 ʽΟ ἐνσώματος λόγος.
= 37 × 57 The Word Incarnate.

Χριστὸς · ʼΑληθὴς λόγος.
Christ : True Word.

ʽΟ λόγος · Κύριος ʼΑδωναί.
The Word : Lord : Adonai.

ʽΥιὸς · Τὸ πλήρωμα.
A Son : the Fulness.

ʽΥιὸς μονογενὴς παρὰ Πατρός.
Only-begotten Son of the Father.

ʽΥιός Βασιλεὺς Παρθενογενής.
A Son : King Virgin-born.

ʽΥιὸς Πατρὸς · ʽΟ ὁμόκληρος.
Son of the Father : the Joint-heir.

ʽΟ Ναζωραῖος · Κύριος.
    The Nazarene : Lord.

Κληρονόμος τῆς βασιλείας Θεοῦ.
    Heir of the Kingdom of God.

ʽΟ Μεσσίας · Σημεῖον Κυρίου.
    The Messiah : Sign of the Lord.

Ὑιὸς Δαβίδ · Σωτήρ.
    Son of David : Saviour.

Φωνὴ Πατρός.
    Voice of the Father.

Γνῶσις καὶ ζωή.
    Knowledge and Life.

Τὸ αὐγοειδὲς σῶμα.
    The Radiant Body. (Gnostic.)

2146   Α · Ω · Ἀρχὴ καὶ τέλος.
= 37 × 58   First : Last : Beginning and End.   (Titles of
                    Christ. Rev.)

Α · Ω · Ἀμὴν · ʽΟ μονογενὴς Ὑιός.
    First : Last : Amen : the Only-begotten Son.

Ἄλφα · Ω · Εἷς Θεὸς δίκαιος.
    First : Last : One Righteous God.

Ἄλφα · Ω · ʽΟ ἐνεργὴς λόγος.
    First : Last : the Powerful Word.

Ἄλφα · Ὤμεγα · Ἄρνιον Θεοῦ.
    First : Last : Lamb of God.   (Rev. vi. 8.)

ʽΗ ἀρχὴ · Τὸ πλήρωμα.
The Beginning : the Fullness.

ʽΗ ζωὴ ἀκατάλυτος.
    The Endless Life.   (Heb. vii. 16.)

Ἰησοῦς ὁ λειτουργός.
    Jesus, the Minister.

ʽΟ ζῶν · ὁ Λόγος ἐκ Πατρός.
    The Living One : the Word from the Father.

Ζῶν Θεὸς ἀνδρῶν.
Living God of Men.

Χαρὶς Θεοῦ Πατρός.
Grace of God the Father.

Ἡ Θεότης ἐκ τοῦ Πατρός.
The Godhead from the Father.

Οἱ Ἀπόστολοι Θεοῦ Πατρός.
The Apostles of God the Father.

Ἁλιεῖς ἀνθρώπων.
Fishers of Men.

Οἱ αἰῶνες Κυρίου.
The Aeons of the Lord.

2183 Κεφάλη ὑπὲρ πάντα τῇ ἐκκλησίᾳ.
= 37 × 59 Head over All to the Church.   (Ep. Eph. i, 22.)

Ἡ βασιλεία τοῦ πνεύματος.
The Kingdom of the Spirit.

Ἡ δύναμις τῆς Θεότητος.
The Power of the Godhead.

Ὁ Θεός · Βασιλεὺς σοφίας.
God the King of Wisdom.

Ὁ θρόνος · Ἰησοῦς ὁ Μεσσίας.
The Throne : Jesus the Messiah.

Ὁ Ὑιὸς Δαβὶδ · Βασιλεὺς ἐκκλησίας.
The Son of David : King of the Church.

Ὑιὸς ἐκ Παρθένου · Μεσίτης.
Son of a Virgin : Mediator.

Ὁ ἐκ παρθένου Λόγος Κυρίου.
The Word of the Lord from a Virgin.

Χριστὸς ὁ Ἅγιος Ἰσραήλ.
Christ the Holy One of Israel.

Ὁ ἀληθὴς λόγος Θεοῦ Κυρίου.
The True Word of the Lord God.

Βαπτίσμα · Μέγα φῶς.
    Baptism : a Great Light.

Λόγος Πατρός · Πλήρωμα.
    Word of the Father : Fulness.

Ἰησούς · Διαθήκη Θεοῦ Πατρός.
    Jesus : Covenant of God the Father.

Εἷς Θεὸς δίκαιος · Θεὸς μόνος ἐκ μόνου.
    One Just God : Only God of Only God.

2220   Ἰησοῦς · Ἄλφα · Ω.
= 37 × 60   Jesus : First : Last.

Α καὶ Ω · Λόγος ζωῆς.
    First and Last : Word of Life.

Α · Ω · Σωτηρία.
    First : Last : Salvation.

Ἀπ᾽ ἀρχῆς ἐξουσία Θεοῦ.
    Authority of God from the Beginning.

Ζῶν ἀπ᾽ ἀρχῆς λόγος.
    Living Word from the Beginning.

Ὁ ζῶν λόγος · ῾Ο ὤν.
    The Living Word : " That I am."

Ὁ ἀόρατος σωτήρ.
    The Saviour Unmanifest.

Ὁ κόκκος τοῦ σίτου.
    The Grain of Wheat.   (Parables.)

Τὰ ἀλεύρου σατὰ τρία.
    The Three Measures of Meal.   740 " 740 " 740.

Ὁ ἐρχόμενος Θεὸς · ὁ Μεσσίας.
    The God that shall come : the Messiah.

2257   Τὸ σωτήριον Ἰσραήλ.
= 37 × 61   The Salvation of Israel.

Εὐαγγέλιον Χριστοῦ.
    Gospel of Christ.

Κιβωτὸς Νωέ.
> Ark of Noah.

Σαλὴμ ἡ χρυσοῦς.
> Salem the Golden.

Οἰκία πνεύματος Κυρίου.
'Ο θρόνος Κυρίου 'Ιησοῦ.
> The Throne of the Lord Jesus.

'Η δύναμις ἡ πᾶσα τοῦ Θεοῦ.
> All the Power of God.

Τὸ Ἀρνίον · 'Η μυστικὴ θυσία.
> The Lamb : the mystic Sacrifice.

Μεσίτης ἐκκλησίας Κυρίου.
> Mediator of the Church of the Lord.

Αἶμα Κυρίου · Ἀρνίον ἐσφαγμένον.
> Blood of the Lord : the Lamb that was slain.

'Ο ἔνσαρκος Κύριος · ὅ Ἀρτος.
> The Incarnate Lord : the Bread.

'Ιησοῦς ἡ Θυσία · 'Ο Ἀρτος.
> Jesus the Sacrifice : the Bread.

2294 Πλήρωμα Θεοῦ Πατρός.
= 37 × 62 Fulness of God the Father.

'Ιησοῦς ἐν σώματι.
> Jesus in the Flesh.

Πρωτότοκος Θεός.
> First-begotten God.

'Υιὸς Θεοῦ ὁμοούστος.
> Son of same Substance with God.

'Η μυστικὴ θυσία 'Ιησοῦ.
> The Mystic Sacrifice of Jesus.

Καὶ τὸ αἶμα μου ἀληθὴς ἐστὶ πόσις.
> "And My blood is drink indeed."

Κηφᾶς ὁ λίθος πνευματικός.
    Cephas the spiritual Stone.

Κύριος Θεὸς ὁ ἐρχόμενος.
    Lord God that shall come.

Σημεῖον Θεοῦ ζῶντος.
    Sign of the Living God.

Ἡ Πίστις τῆς ἐκκλησίας Θεοῦ.
    The Faith of the Church of God.

Πίστις ἐκκλησίας Κυρίου
    Faith of the Church of the Lord.

Ἰησοῦς ὁ Ὑιὸς Μεσσίας.
    Jesus, the Son : Messiah.

Χριστὸς ὁ ἐνεργὴς Λόγος.
    Christ the powerful Word.

2331   Ἄλφα καὶ ὤμεγα · Ὄνομα Ἰησοῦ.
= 37 × 63   First and Last : Name of Jesus.

Α · Ω · Ἀμὴν · Ὑιὸς Πατρός.
    First : Last : Amen : Son of the Father.

Παράκλητος τοῦ Πατρός.
    Paraclete, of the Father.

Μέγας Παράκλητος μονογενὴς ἐκ Πατρός.
    Great Paraclete Only-begotten of the Father

Τὸ πᾶν πνεῦμα τοῦ Θεοῦ.
    The All-Spirit of God.

Τὸ Πνεῦμα κατάβαινον · Ὁ Παράκλητος.
    The Spirit Descending : the Paraclete.

Ἰησοῦς ὁ Λόγος Κυρίου.
    Jesus the Word of the Lord.

Οὐσία τοῦ Ὑιοῦ.
    Substance of the Son.

Χριστὸς Ὕπαρξις.
    Christ the Substance.

2368 Ἰησοῦς Χριστός.
= 37 × 64   Ὁ Ἅγιος τῶν Ἁγίων.
       (For rest, see published lists.)

Μεγαλης βούλης ἄγγελος · Πλήρωμα.
       Councillor (title of Messiah. Isaiah ix) : Fulness.

2405 Ὁ Λόγος Θεοῦ · Ὁ Σωτήρ.
= 37 × 65   The Word of God : the Saviour.

Ὁ Σωτὴρ ὁ Ζῶν.
       The Living Saviour.

Λόγος Πατρός · Ὁ Θεὸς ὁ Ζῶν.
       The Word of the Father : the Living God.

Λόγος τῆς ἀληθείας ἐκ Θεοῦ Πατρός.
       Word of Truth from God the Father.

Λόγος ἔσχατος · Μεσσίας.
       Word of the Last : Messiah.

Θεὸς ἀληθινὸς ἐκ Θεοῦ ἀληθινοῦ · Μεσσίας.
       Very God of Very God : Messiah.

Ἡ διδαχὴ τοῦ Κυρίου.
       The Teaching of the Lord.

Τὸ εὐαγγέλιον τοῦ Ἰησοῦ.
       The Gospel of Jesus.

Βασιλεία πνευμάτος Κυρίου.
       Kingdom of the Spirit of the Lord

Ἡ σαγήνη τῆς σωτηρίας.
       The Net of Salvation.

Ἀληθὴς λόγος ἐκ Κυρίου Πατρός.
       True Word of the Lord the Father

2442 Ἡ ἐξουσία Κυρίου Ἰησοῦ.
= 37 × 66   The Authority of the Lord Jesus.

Υἱὸς Θεοῦ · Δύναμις Λόγου.
       Son of God : Power of the Word.

Ἰησους · Μόνος Λόγος Πατρός.
       Jesus Only Word of the Father.

Κήρυγμα φῶτος
> Preaching of Light.

Ἡ διαμεριζομένη γλῶσσα πυρός.
> The Cloven Tongue of Fire.

Ὁ σπείρων τὸν λόγον Θεοῦ.
> The Sower of the Word of God.

Ἡ γνῶσις ἐκ Πνεύματος.
> The Knowledge from the Spirit.

Λειτουργός τοῦ Θεοῦ.
> Minister of God.

Καλὴ δύναμις Σωτῆρος.
> Good Power of the Saviour.

Ὁ Ὑιὸς · Θεὸς Σωτήρ.
> The Son : God the Saviour.

Χριστὸς · "Ορασις Εἰρήνης.
> Christ the Beatific Vision.

2479   Ἀστὴρ φῶτος.
= 37 × 67   Star of Light.

Πλήρωμα · Ὁ λύχνος.
> Pleroma : the Lamp.

Ἡ ὅδος τῆς σωτηρίας.
> The Way of Salvation.

Ἀποκάλυψις τῆς βασιλείας.
> Revelation of the Kingdom.

"Αλφα · "Ωμεγα · ἡ Ἐκπόρευσις.
> First : Last : the " Procession."

Α · Ω · Ὁ Λόγος Θεοῦ Πατρός.
> First : Last : Word of God the Father.

2516   Ἐξουσία τοῦ Κυρίου.
= 37 × 68   Authority of the Lord.

Χριστὸς ἡ πᾶσα ἐξουσία.
> Christ the Full Authority.

Ἡ πᾶσα δύναμις τοῦ Πατρός.
The Whole Power of the Father.

Ἡ βάπτισις · Δύναμις Κυρίου.
Baptism : Power of the Lord.

Ἅγιον μυστήριον βαπτίσματος.
Holy Mystery of Baptism.

Ἡ ἄφεσις ἁμαρτίων ἡ πᾶσα.
The Total Taking-away of Sins.

Ἡ δύναμις λόγου ἀφίεναι ἁμαρτίας.
The Power of the Word for the Taking away
of Sin.

Ἡ δίδαξις τῆς ἀφέσεως.
The Teaching of the Cleansing.

Τέκνον, ἀφίενται σοῦ αἱ ἅμάρτιαι.
"Son, thy sins are forgiven"; a reason for
reading ἀφίενῖαι.

Ἡ ἐλπὶς · Ἡ δύναμις τῆς Θεότητος.
The Hope : the Power of the Godhead.

Ἡ διαθήκη τοῦ Σωτῆρος.
The Covenant of the Saviour.

Ἀληθινὸς Λυτρωτής.
True Deliverer or Redeemer.

Χώρα ζωῆς.
Land of Life (Gnostic Books).

Σημεῖον τοῦ βαπτιστοῦ.
Sign of the Baptist.

Χάραγμα τοῦ Κυρίου.
The Lord's Mark.

Χ · Μ · Γ · Λόγος κατὰ μυστήριον.
(See diagram. Book of Ieou.)

Υἱὸς Πατρός · Μόνος ἐκ μόνου.

Ὁ μονογενὴς Θεὸς ἐνσώματος.

2553 Ὑιός · Λόγος κατὰ μυστήριον.
= 37 × 69   A Son : Word according to the Mystery.

Σημεῖον Θεοῦ εἰς τὴν γνῶσιν.
    Sign of God unto Knowledge.

Ἡ πᾶσα γνῶσις Κυρίου.
    The All-Knowledge of the Lord.

Ἡ γνῶσις · Ἡ ἰδέα τοῦ Θεοῦ.
    The Gnosis : the Idea of God.

Ἡ Σοφία · Ἡ κλῖμαξ τοῦ Ἰακώβ.
    Wisdom : Jacob's Ladder.

Βαπτίσμα · Τὸ μέγα φῶς.
    Baptism : the Great Light.

2590 Μυστικὸν φῶς.
= 37 × 70   Mystic Light.

Μυστικὸς λύχνος.
    Mystic Lamp.

Τόπος φῶτος.
    Place of Light.

Ἡ σφαῖρα τοῦ Κυρίου.
    The Sphere of the Lord.

Χριστὸς · Ὑιὸς μόνος.
    Christ : Only Son.

Δωρεὰ Χριστου.
    Gift of Christ (Baptism).

Α καὶ Ω · Ὁ Κύριος Ἰησοῦς.
    First and Last : the Lord Jesus

Χριστὸς ἡ δόξα τῆς βασιλείας.
    Christ the Glory of the Kingdom.

Ὁ λόγος · Ἡ Εἰκὼν τοῦ Θεοῦ.
    The Word : Image of God.

Τὰ πάντα καὶ ἐν πᾶσι Χριστός.
    Christ All and In All.

Α · Ω · Ἡ σοφία Κυρίου.
    First : Last : the Wisdom of the Lord.

2627 Λόγος τοῦ Θεοῦ Κυρίου.
= 37 × 71 Word of the Lord God.

Λόγος ἐκ Πατρός ὁ Σωτήρ.
Word from the Father : the Saviour.

Λόγος Κυρίου · Ὁ ἀμὴν · Μόνος ἐκ μόνου.

Λόγος Κυρίου · Ἐμμανουὴλ ὁ διδάσκαλος.
Word of the Lord : Emmanuel the Teacher.

Ἀλφα καὶ Ὠμεγα · Ὁ λόγος τῆς ἀληθείας.
First and Last : the Word of Truth.

Ἄλφα · Ὠμεγα · Ὁ μονογενὴς Ὑιός.
First : Last : the Only-begotten Son.

Α καὶ Ω · Τὸ ἔνταλμα Κυρίου.
First : Last : the Command of the Lord.

Α · Ω · Τὸ Πνεῦμα · Ὁ Παράκλητος.
First : Last : the Spirit : the Comforter.

Α · Ω · Ἀμὴν · Ὁ ζῶν Κύριος.
First : Last : Amen : the Living Lord.

Ἀρχὴ καὶ Τέλος · Ἡ γένεσις · Α · Ω.
Beginning and End : the Beginning : First : Last.

Ἀρχὴ καὶ Τέλος · Ἀπάτωρ.
Beginning and End : without Father.

Ἀρχὴ καὶ Τέλος · Λόγος ἀρχής.
Beginning and End : Word of the Beginning.

Α · Ω · Ἀμὴν · Θεὸς · ὁ Λόγος Κυρίου.
First : Last : Amen : God : the Word of the
Lord.

Α · Ω · Κύριος Θεὸς ἀόρατος.
First : Last : Lord God Invisible.

Α · Ω · Ἀμὴν · Ὁ μέγας Σωτήρ.
First : Last : Amen : the Great Saviour.

Ἄλφα · Ὠμεγα · Θεὸς · Τριὰς τέλεια.
First : Last : God : Perfect Trinity.

2627 Τὸ εὐαγγέλιον Χριστοῦ.
= 37 × 71   The Gospel of Christ.

 Ὁ Νόμος σωτηρίας.
  The Law of Salvation.

 Ὁ Κύριος · Σωτὴρ Ἰσραήλ.
  The Lord : Saviour of Israel.

 Σωτὴρ καὶ Λειτουργός.
  Saviour and Minister.

 Ι · Χ · Θ · Υ · Σ · Σωτήρ.
  Icthys : Saviour.

 Εὐχαριστία Κυρίου.
  The Lord's Eucharist.

 Ὁ Ἄρτος ἐκ τοῦ οὐρανοῦ.
  The Bread from Heaven.

2664 Τὸ Πλήρωμα Θεοῦ Πατρός.
= 37 × 72   The Fulness of God the Father.

 Ἰησοῦς · Ἡ Ἀρχὴ · Πλήρωμα.
  Jesus, the Beginning : Fulness.

 Φῶς · Υἱὸς Θεοῦ.
  Light : Son of God.

 Υἱὸς Θεοῦ κατὰ μυστήριον.
  Son of God according to the Mystery.

 Φῶς · Δύναμις βασιλείας.
  Light : Power of the Kingdom.

 Φῶς · Ἡ μάθησις Ἰησοῦ.
  Light : The Teaching of Jesus.

2701 Κύριος τοῦ αἰῶνος.
= 37 × 73   Lord of the Aeon.

 Μόνος Κύριος οὐρανῶν.
  Only Lord of the Heavens.

 Ζῶν Λόγος Σταύρου.
  Living Word of the Cross.

 Ὁ Αἰὼν τοῦ Κυρίου.
  The Lord's Aeon.

ʿΟ μέγας αἰὼν τοῦ Πατρός.
The Great Aeon of the Father.

ʿΗ Ἀρχὴ · Φῶς Θεοῦ.
The Beginning : Light of God.

Ἄλφα καὶ Ὠμεγα · ʿΟ Ἰχθύς.
First and Last : the Icthys.

2738 Βασιλεὺς ἀνθρώπων.
= 37 × 74 King of Men.

ʿΟ μέγας Κύριος σωτηρίας.
The Great Lord of Salvation.

ʿΥιὸς γνώσεως.
Son of Knowledge.

Γνῶσις · Τέκτων.
Gnosis : the Builder.

2775 ʿΗ ἐνανθρώπησις τοῦ Θεοῦ.
= 37 × 75 The Incarnation of God in Man.

Τὸ Ἀρνιον · Σῶμα καὶ Αἷμα Κυρίου.
The Lamb : the Lord's Flesh and Blood.

Λόγος καὶ Δύναμις ἐνσώματος.
Word and Power Incarnate.

Τὸ Μυστήριον τὸ ζῶν.
The Living Mystery.

Ζῶν Λόγος · ʿΟ Τέκτων.
Living Word : the Builder.

ʿΟ Ἀρτος Θεοῦ · ʿΟ Χριστός.
Bread of God : the Christ.

Ἀρχικώτατος Λόγος.
Word Most Supreme (Title of Christ).
Clem. Al.

Γεωμετρία κατὰ τὴν Σοφίαν.
Geometry according to the Wisdom.

2812   Τὸ Σημεῖον τοῦ Ἰχθύος.
= 37 × 76   Sign of the Fish.

Αὐτόσωμα Κυρίου.
  Very Body of the Lord.

Σὰρξ καὶ Αἷμα Ἰησοῦ Χριστοῦ.
  Flesh and Blood of Jesus Christ.

Ὁ ἐκπορευόμενος Λόγος τοῦ Θεοῦ.
  The Word proceeding from God.

Αλφα · Ὤμεγα · Υἱὸς Πατρός.
  First : Last : Son of the Father.

Λόγος Θεοῦ · Ὁ μέλλων ἔρχεσθαι.
  Word of God : He that shall come.

Υἱὸς τοῦ Παντοκράτορος.
  Son of the Omnipotent.

Ὁ Ὤν · Ὁ Παντοκράτωρ.
  He Who Is : the Almighty.

Χριστὸς · Ἄλφα · Ω·
  Christ : First : Last.

2849   Ὁ Λόγος Κυρίου ἐν σώματι.
= 37 × 77   The Word of the Lord Incarnate.

Ζῶν Λόγος σωτηρίας.
  Living Word of Salvation.

Λόγος προφορικὸς τῆς ἀληθείας Θεοῦ.
  Uttered Word of the Truth of God.

Λόγος εἰρήνης · Σωτὴρ καὶ Μεσσίας.
  Word of Peace : Saviour and Messiah.

Υἱὸς καὶ Λυτρωτής.
  Son and Ransomer.

Τὰ μυστήρια τῆς σοφίας.
  The Mysteries of Wisdom.

Κληρονομία τοῦ Χριστοῦ.
  Inheritance of Christ.

2886 Χρηστὸς Σωτήρ.
= 37 × 78   Good Saviour.

Χριστὸς ἐν σώματι.
　Christ in the Flesh.

Ἰησοῦς ὁ Ὑιὸς ἐκ τῆς Παρθένου.
　Jesus, the Son of the Virgin.

Ζῶν Λόγος τοῦ Θεοῦ καὶ ἐνεργής (*see* Ep. Heb iv, 12).
　Quick and Powerful Word of God.

Ἰησοῦς Μεσίτης Θεοῦ Πατρός.
　Jesus, Mediator of God the Father.

Χριστὸς ὁ Ὑιὸς · Μεσσίας.
　Christ the Son : Messiah.

Ὁ μακάριος καὶ μόνος Δυνάστης · Ο Ὑιός.
　The Son, the Blessed and Only Potentate.

Ὁ Θεὸς Σωτήρ · Λόγος Πατρός.
　God the Saviour : Word of the Father.

Ὁ Σωτήρ · Ἡ πέτρα πνευματική.
　The Saviour : the Spiritual Rock.

Ζῶν Κύριος · Βασιλεὺς εἰρήνης.
　Living Lord : King of Peace.

Βασιλεὺς Σαλήμ · Ὁ Κύριος τῆς εἰρήνης.
　King of Salem : the Lord of Peace.

Μελχισεδὲκ ἡ Δύναμις τοῦ Θεοῦ.
　Melchisedec, the Power of God.

Μέγας Σωτήρ · Βασιλεὺς εἰρήνης.
　Great Saviour : King of Peace.

Ἡ παρρησία καὶ τὸ καύχημα τῆς ἐλπίδος.
　"The confidence and rejoicing of the Hope."

2923   Α · Ω · Ἐμμανουήλ · Ὁ Σωτήρ.
= 37 × 79   First : Last : Emmanuel the Saviour.

Ὁ Μεσσίας · Ὁ Σωτήρ τῆς γῆς.
　The Messiah : the Saviour of the Earth.

Χριστὸς ὁ Λόγος Κυρίου.
　Christ, the Word of the Lord.

168 *The Apostolic Gnosis.*

Ζῶν Κύριος · Εἰκὼν εἰρήνης.
Living Lord : Image of Peace.

Ο Μεσσίας ὁ Σωτὴρ · Ὁ Ποιμὴν ὁ καλός.
The Messiah, the Saviour : the Good Shepherd.

Ο Λόγος Κυρίου · Ἄλφα · Ὤμεγα · Ἀμὴν.
The Word of the Lord : Alpha : Omega : Amen.

Ὑιὸς Μαρίας · Κύριος οὐρανοῦ.
Son of Mary : Lord of Heaven.

Ἰησοῦς ἡ δικαιοσύνη τοῦ Θεοῦ.
Jesus, the Righteousness of God.

Ἰησοῦς · Σοφία τοῦ Θεοῦ.
Jesus : Wisdom of God.

Ἡ ἐκκλησία τῶν οὐρανῶν.
The Church of the Heavens.

Ἡ γνῶσις κατὰ Χριστόν.
The Knowledge according to Christ.

Παραμύθιον λαῶν πάντων.
Consolation of all Nations.

Τὸ μέγα Φῶς · Τὸ Βάπτισμα.
The Great Light : the Baptism.

2960 Ἰησοῦς Χριστὸς Θεότης.
= 37 × 80 Jesus Christ : Godhead.

Θεότης Ἰησοῦ Χριστοῦ.
Godhead of Jesus Christ.

Ὑιὸς τοῦ Ἀνθρώπου.
Son of Man. (Autonym of Jesus.)

Ὁ Κύριος ἀνθρωπόμορφος.
The Lord in Human Form.

Χριστὸς Ὑιὸς Κύριος.
Christ : Son : Lord.

Ὁ Κύριος ὁ Ῥυόμενος ἐκ Σιών.
The Lord : the Deliverer out of Sion.

Ἰησοῦς · Τὸ Ἄλφα · Τὸ Ω.
Jesus : the First and Last.

'Ιησοῦς·'Η γνῶσις Α · Ω.
Jesus : the Gnosis : A. O.

Χριστὸς· Τὸ ἀληθινὸν Πάσχα.
Christ : the True Passover.

῎Ελευσις τοῦ 'Ερχομένου.
The Advent of Him Who shall come.

Πλήρωμα τοῦ αἰῶνος.
Fulness of the Aeon.

'Αυτοδύναμις Θεοῦ Κυρίου.
Very Power of the Lord God.

'Ασαλευτὸς θρόνος τοῦ θεοῦ.
Unshaken Throne of God.

Κύριος ἐκκλησίας ἐνσώματος.
Incarnate Lord of the Church.

Χριστὸς · Καινὴ φιλοσοφία.
Christ, the New Philosophy.

Φῶς τῆς ἀληθείας 'Ιησοῦ.
Light of the Truth of Jesus.

Τὸ μυστικὸν Φῶς.
The Mystic Light.

Μυστικὴ ἐκκλησία Κυρίου 'Ιησοῦ.
Mystical Church of the Lord Jesus.

Γνῶσις·'Ο Λόγος τοῦ Θεοῦ.
Gnosis, the Word of God.

'Η 'Αληθογνωσία τοῦ Κυρίου.
The True Knowledge of the Lord.

'Εκπόρευσις Φῶτος.
" Procession " of Light.

Τὸ 'Εκπόρευμα· ῎Οψις τῆς εἰρήνης.
The Procession : Beatific Vision.

Τὸ θεῖον πνεῦμα φῶτος.
The Divine Spirit of Light.

Φῶς ἀθάνατον ἐκκλησίας Θεοῦ.
Immortal Light of the Church of God.

Ἥλιος δικαιοσύνης· ὁ μέγας λύχνος.
Sun of Righteousness : the Great Light.

Τὸ μυστικὸν ὄρος Σιών.
The Mystical Mount Sion.

Ἐκκλησία τῶν ἡγιασμένων Ἰσραήλ.
Church of the Elect of Israel.

Κατασκεύασις Κιβωτοῦ.
Preparing of the Ark.

Τὸ αἶμα τῆς διαθήκης τοῦ Κυρίου.
The Blood of the Covenant of the Lord.

Ζωὴ· Μυστήριον τῆς βασιλείας.
Life : the Mystery of the Kingdom.

Πίστις Σοφία· Γνῶσις ἀληθινὴ.
Faith, Wisdom : True Gnosis.

Ἡ Ἀρχὴ· Λόγος φῶτος.
The Beginning : Word of Light.

Θεότης Θεοτήτος ἐν σώματι.
Godhead of Godhead in the Flesh.

Θεότης ἐν σώματι· Ὅρασις εἰρήνης.
Godhead in the Flesh : Vision of Peace.

Θεότης ἐν σώματι· Τριὰς τέλεια.
Godhead in the Flesh : Perfect Trinity.

Μεσσίας ἡμῶν ἐν σώματι.
Our Messiah in the Flesh.

Μόνος Λόγος Πατρὸς ἐν σώματι.
Only Word of the Father in the Flesh.

Ἀληθὴς Λόγος ἐν σώματι Μεσσίου.
True Logos in the Body of the Messiah.

Ἰησοῦς Λόγος ἀγάπης ἐν σώματι.
Jesus, Logos of Love in the Body.

Ὁ λόγος ἐν σώματι καὶ τὸ Ἅγιον Πνεῦμα.
The Word Incarnate and the Holy Spirit.

Λόγος εἰρήνης· Κύριος ἐν σώματι.
Logos of Peace : Lord in the Flesh.

Λόγια ζῶντα Κυρίου Ἰησοῦ.
Living Words of the Lord Jesus.

Λόγος μυστήριου · Μέγας Παράκλητος (or Πλήρωμα).
Word of the Mystery : Great Paraclete (or Fulness).

Λόγος ἐκ τοῦ Πνεύματος ἔνσαρκος.
Word Incarnate from the Spirit.

Θεὸς ἔνσαρκος ἐκ τοῦ Θεοῦ Πατρός.
God Incarnate from God the Father.

Σοφία · Ὁ Λόγος ὁ ἐνσώματος.
Wisdom : the Word Incarnate.

Πρόσωπον Ἀνθρωποῦ.
Person of a Man.

Ἡ Γεωμετρία Κυρίου Ἰησοῦ.
The Geometry of the Lord Jesus.

Ὁ Γεωμέτρης : Μονογενὴς παρὰ Πατρός.
The Geometrician : Only-begotten of the Father.

Ὁ Νόμος τῆς ἀληθείας Κυρίου Ἰησοῦ.
The Law of the Truth of the Lord Jesus.

Ὁ Μεσίτης τῆς Σωτηρίας.
The Mediator of Salvation.

Ἰησοῦς Κύριος · Μονογενὴς ἐκ Πατρὸς.
Jesus : Lord, Only-begotten of the Father.

Ἰησοῦς ὁ Ναζωραῖος · Μεσίτης.
Jesus the Nazarene : Mediator.

Εἷς Κύριος · Ὑπόστασις Θεοῦ.
One Lord : Substance of God.

Ζῶν Θεὸς · Λίθος κατὰ μυστήριον.
Living God : Stone according to the Mystery.

Σημεῖον σωτηρίας · Ὁ Ἰησοῦς.
Sign of Salvation : Jesus.

Χριστὸς · Μεσσίας · Ὁ Λόγος εἰρήνης.
Christ : Messiah : Word of Peace.

Μεσσίας · ὁ Θεὸς ὁ ὕψιστὸς.
The Messiah : the Highest God.

Ἰησοῦς · Κύριος · Μεσίτης ἐκ Θεοῦ.
 Jesus : Lord : Mediator from God.

Σωτὴρ Κόσμου · Νομοθετής·
 Saviour of the World : Lawgiver.

Ἰχθὺς ·'Ο "Αρτος Κυρίου.
 Fish : the Bread of the Lord.

Ὁ Μεσσίας ·'Η Δύναμις τοῦ Πατρός.
 The Messiah : the Power of the Father.

Metacube *a.*   37 × 80 = 2960.   Ἡ Γεωμετρία Κυρίου Ἰησοῦ.
      b.   19 × 80 = 1520.   Ἐκκλησία τῆς Μητρός.
                             Πνεῦμα Θεοτόκου.
                             Πνεῦμα ἀληθείας + Υἱὸς.
                              (152 = Μάρια.)

      56 × 80 = 4480.   Χριστὸς Φῶς κατὰ μυστήριον.

Inner Cube.   8 × 80 = 640.

      64 × 80 = 5120 = 8 × 8 × 8 × 10.

      Ἰησοῦς Χριστὸς ἡ μορφὴ τῆς ἀληθείας τοῦ Θεοῦ.

      Γνῶσις τῆς σοφίας Ἰησοῦ Χριστοῦ.

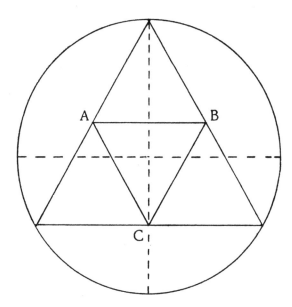

In this diagram the following are the approximate measures, with their gematria.

1. Radius of Circle $= 1480 = $ Χριστὸς.

2. Diameter of Circle $= 2960$
   $= $ Ὑιὸς τοῦ Ἀνθρώπου. (Son of Man.)

3. Circumference of Circle $= 9300$ in gematria 930·0.
   $= $ Θεὸς Ἐνσαρκὸς. (God Incarnate.)

4. Cross diameters $= 5920$ in gematria 592·0.
   $= $ Θεοτὴς. (Deity : Godhead.)

5. Perimeter of Triangle
   ABC in circle, its sides
   being each 1282 nearly
   in length $= 3846$
   $= $ Ἰησοῦς Χριστὸς ὁ Σωτὴρ. (Jesus Christ the Saviour.)

The larger Triangle has sides double the length, each being 2564, the gematria for which is Ἀληθεία Κυρίου κατὰ μυστήριον.

2997 'Ο Κύριος τῆς σωτηρίας.
= 37 × 81   The Lord of Salvation.

'Ο Σωτήρ · Κύριος τῆς γῆς.
   The Saviour : Lord of the Earth.

'Ο Σωτὴρ τοῦ γενοῦς Δαβίδ.
   The Saviour of the Race of David.

Η σωτηρία τοῦ κόσμου.
   The Salvation of the World.

Τὸ ἔνδυμα τῆς σωτηρίας.
   The Garment of Salvation.

37 × 81 is 37 × 3 × 3 × 3 × 3, and therefore a Fourth
Power. As such it symbolises the transcendent functions
of aeonial geometry in which the Five-pointed Star, the
Mystery of the Five Words, is a typical illustration. With
this we may again connect the idea of the Stone, and the
teaching of the Metacube and of Cephas as a power of
God in manifestation. The Gematria follows :—

Τὸ πέμπτον σημεῖον σωτηρίας.
   The Fifth Point of Salvation.

'Η πᾶσα γεωμετρία · τὸ Πεντέρημα Θεοῦ.
   The All-geometry : the Five-word (mystery)
      of God.

Κηφᾶς ὁ Πέτρος · τὸ Πεντέρημα Θεοῦ.
   Cephas the Stone.

῎Αλας κυβόμορφον · τὸ Πεντέρημα Θεοῦ.
   Rock-salt.

Κηφᾶς ὁ Πέτρος · ὁ Δόμος ἐπὶ τὴν πέτραν.
   Cephas the Stone : the House upon the Rock.

᾿Εκκλησία σωτήρ · Οἴκημα Πνεύματος.
   Saviour Church : Dwelling of the Spirit.

'Ο τόπος Κυρίου ἀσάλευτος.
   The Unshaken Place of the Lord.

Χριστὸς · Πέτρος ὁ Κύβος.
   Christ : Peter the Cube.

Κεφάλη γωνίας · Εἰκὼν Θεοῦ.
> Head of the Corner : Image of God.

Λίθος σωτηρίας · Πλήρωμα.
> Stone of Salvation : Fulness.

Ὁ λίθος τῆς γωνίας · ἡ πᾶσα ἐξουσία.
> Stone of the Corner : the All-Authority.

Κυβικὸς πέτρος · ἡ πᾶσα ἐξουσία Θεοῦ.
> A cubic Stone : the All-Authority of God.

Λόγος Κυρίου · Δύναμις Μελχισεδέκ.
> Word of the Lord : Power of Melchisedek.

Χριστός · Δύναμις καὶ Σοφία.
> Christ : Power and Wisdom.

Ἰησοῦς ὁ ἐνσώματος Λόγος.
> Jesus the Word Incarnate.

Ὁ οἶκος τοῦ τέκτονος τῆς ἀληθείας.
> The House of the Builder of Truth.

Ζῶν Λόγος ἐκ Θεοῦ · ὁ Λειτουργός.
> Living Word from God : the Minister.

Ἰεου · ὁ Λειτουργός τοῦ Θεοῦ.
> ΙΕΟΥ : the Minister of God.

It is the Minister, the Λειτουργός, who possesses the power to enter within the Veil—that is, in the Gnostic symbology, to penetrate into the Unseen Dimension.

The three Cubes of the Temple, each $10 \times 10 \times 10$, make 3000, but this 3000 appears to be accommodated to the metacubic scale, as we find demonstrated elsewhere with sufficient clearness. It thus becomes 2997, or 3×999. Thus one of these cubes is Ἱερεὺς Σαλήμ $= 999$. Now the edge, or cube root, of 2997 is 14·42 nearly, and this quantity is taken in the published Tables as the Cube Root of Three, viz. 1·442. In the gematria 1442 is the τέταρτον ἄπειρον, the Fourth Boundless Line. But at a higher evaluation which again equates it with the Meta-cubic Scale, it will be 1443 = Ὁ Λόγος Κυρίου. But take it as 1442 (14·42). The Square on this is 208·2 or 208·3 (2083 in gematria). And this is the hypersolidity of the Penterema figure whose edge is that of a cube of 100·000. The gematria of 2083 is Μυστήριον Πεντέρημα ἄπειρον.— The Infinite Five-Word Mystery.

So now we have got the root of the Temple gematria. For if the edge of the Penterema be 1443 = ὁ Λόγος Κυρίου, then the square faces are each 2083 by gematria = Μυστήριον πεντέρημα ἄπειρον, and the six faces will total 1250 (2×5^4) = Θρόνος Πατρός.

The solidity of the cube can be got by multiplying 1442 by itself twice : as we have said, 14·42 is the scale to be adopted. And the cube of 14·42 works out at 2997. So 2997 becomes our cubic temple.

And the tesseract is represented by the figures 132-133, in reality representing a function of root 3, but as we find in gematria, preferred as 432 usually for a cosmic measure, 4326 = 3 × 1442.

3034 Ὁ μέγας Θεὸς τῶν πάντων.
= 37 × 82 Great God of All.

  Κύριος Θεὸς ὁ ὕψιστος.
  Lord God the Highest.

  Φῶς · ἀστὴρ Μεσσίου.
  Light : Star of the Messiah.

  Χριστὸς Μεσσίας ἡμῶν.
  Christ Our Messiah.

  Ἀστὴρ Θεοῦ · φέγγος πρώινον.
  Star of God : Morning Radiance (*cf.* Job xxxviii. 12).

And hundreds of other combinations, as ὁ οἶκος Κυρίου ὁ ἀχειροποίητος. The House not made with hands.

3071 Ὑιὸς Κυρίου προαιώνιος.
= 37 × 83 Son of God before the Aeons (see Rendel Harris' Testimonies, p. 15).

Ὁ Σωτὴρ · μόνος δυνάστης.
The Saviour : Only Potentate.

Τὸ πλήρωμα · μονὰς πάντων.
The Fulness : One of All.

Ἡ θύρα τῶν προβάτων.
The Door of the Sheep.
(Type of Christ, S. John x. 7).

3108   Φῶς · λόγος Θεοῦ Πατρός.
= 37 × 84   Light : Word of God the Father.

Λόγος Θεοῦ πατρός κατὰ μυστήριον.
Τὸ φῶς · ἡ ἐξουσία Θεοῦ.
The Light : the Authority of God.

Φῶς · ἐξουσία τῆς ἡμέρας.
Light : Authority of the Day.

Φῶς · ἐκπόρευσις ἡλίου.
Light : Emanation of the Sun.

Φῶς · διδαχὴ σοφίας.
Light : Teaching of Wisdom.

Φῶς ἡμέρας τοῦ Θεοῦ.
Light of God's Day.

Μυστικὸν φῶς ἡλίου.
Mystic Light of the Sun.

Σωτήριον τοῦ κόσμου.
Salvation of the World.

Σωτηρία γῆς · ὁ Σωτήρ.
Salvation of the World : the Saviour.

Ἡ σωτηρία · Ἰησοῦς · Θεὸς ἐκ Θεοῦ.
The Salvation : Jesus : God of God.

Ἡ σωτηρία Ἰσραὴλ · Θεότης ἐκ παρθένου.
The Salvation of Israel : Godhead from a
Virgin.

Ὑιὸς Μαρίας · ὁ μέγας Σωτὴρ Ἰσραήλ.
Son of Mary : the Great Saviour of Israel.

Ἡ καταβολὴ ἐκ τῆς οὐσίας τοῦ Θεοῦ.
The Conception from the Substance of God.

Δύναμις Θεοῦ πρὸς σωτηρίαν.
Power of God unto Salvation.

Λύχνος ἀναστάσεως.
Lamp of Resurrection.

Ἰησοῦς Κύριος · ὁ λύχνος.
Lord Jesus : the Lamp.

Ὁ Μεσσίας · Αἰὼν τοῦ Πατρός.
The Messiah : Aeon of the Father.

Ἄλφα ·Ὠμεγα · ὁ ζῶν Κύριος.
First : Last : The Living Lord.

Α · Ω · Ἀμὴν · Σωτὴρ κόσμου.
First : Last : Amen : Saviour, &c.

Στερεὰ τροφὴ · γνῶσις ἀληθής.
Strong Meat : True Gnosis.

Ὁ πνευματικὸς λόγος τῆς σοφίας.

3145   Θεὸς τῶν αἰώνων.
= 37 × 85   God of the Aeons.

Ὁ θρόνος ἐν τῷ οὐρανῷ.
The Throne in Heaven.

Κύριος σωτηρίας · ὁ Μεσσίας.
Lord of Salvation : the Messiah.

Κύριος κοσμοῦ · ὁ Τέκτων.
Lord of the Universe : the Builder.

Ζῶν Λόγος Υἱὸς Θεοῦ Πατρός.
Living Word : Son of God the Father.

Ἰησοῦς τὸ σωτήριον Ἰσραήλ.
Jesus the Salvation of Israel.

Α · Ω · Ἀδωναί · ὁ Σωτήρ.
First : Last : Adonai : the Saviour.

Πρόσωπον τοῦ Μεσσίου.
Person of the Messiah.

Λόγος Πατρός · Πλήρωμα θεότητος.
Word of the Father : Fulness of the Godhead.

Χριστὸς · Ἄλφα · Ὠμεγα · Θεός.
Christ : First : Last : God.

3182 Λόγος γνώσεως Πατρός.
= 37 × 86 Word of the Knowledge of the Father.

Ἡ γνῶσις Θεοῦ · ἡ σωτηρία.
The Knowledge of God : Salvation.

Τὸ ἀληθὲς μυστήριον Ἰωάννου.
The True Mystery of John.

Ὁ ἐνεργὴς λόγος Ἰησοῦ Χριστοῦ.
The Powerful Word of Jesus Christ.

Ὁ Ἀστὴρ Χριστοῦ ἐν τῇ ἀνατολῇ.
The Star of Christ in the East.

Μυστήριον · λόγος τοῦ Ἰωνᾶ.
Mystery : Word of Jonah.

Κῆτος · ὁ λόγος ἐνεργὴς τοῦ Κυριοῦ.
A Whale + the Powerful Word of God.

Τὰ ζῶα κυκλόθεν τοῦ θρόνου.
The Beasts around the Throne.

Ὁ Ματθαῖος · ὁ Μάρκος · ὁ Λουκᾶς · ὁ Ἰωάννης.
Matthew : Mark : Luke : John.

3219 Θεὸς ἐκ τῆς οὐσίας τοῦ Πατρός.
= 37 × 87 God of the Substance of the Father.

Χριστὸς Ὑιὸς · Πλήρωμα.
Christ : Son : Fulness.

Κύριος σωτηρίας κόσμου.
Lord of the World's Salvation.

Ὁ Ναζωραῖος · Μεσσίας τοῦ Θεοῦ.
The Nazarene : Messiah of God.

Ὁ ἔσχατος Ἀδάμ ; ὁ ζῶν Κύριος.
The Last Adam : The Living Lord.

Λόγος τῆς ἀρχῆς μονογενὴς παρὰ Πατρός.
Word of the Beginning Only-begotten of the
Father.

Θυσία Ἰησοῦ · μυστικὸς ἄρτος.
Sacrifice of Jesus : Mystic Bread.

3256   Πνεῦμα Κυρίου Χριστοῦ.
= 37 × 88   Spirit of the Lord Christ.

Πνεῦμα ἅγιον ἐκ τοῦ Κυρίου Πατρός.
Holy Spirit from God the Father.

Σημεῖον σωτηρίας τοῦ Θεοῦ.
Sign of the Salvation of God.

Λόγος τοῦ Πατρὸς Παντοκράτορος.
Word of the Father Almighty.

Λόγος κατὰ μυστήριον · Σημεῖον Κυρίου.
Word according to the Mystery : Sign of the
Lord.

Φῶς Θεοῦ · ἡ γεωμετρία.
Light of God : Geometry.

Πλήρωμα θεότητος Θεοῦ Πατρός.
Fulness of the Godhead of God the Father.

Χριστὸς ἡ σωτηρία Ἰσραήλ.
Christ the Salvation of Israel.

Ἰησοῦς ὁ Ἅγιος τῶν Ἁγίων.
Jesus the Holy One of Holy Ones.

Ἡ τελείωσις Κυρίου Ἰησοῦ.
That Perfecting of the Lord Jesus.

3293   Λόγος τοῦ Θεοῦ ἐνσώματος.
= 37 × 89   Word of God Incarnate.

Χριστὸς Κύριος Σαβαώθ.
Christ : Lord of Hosts.

Ἰησοῦς ὁ Λόγος Θεοῦ · ὁ Σωτήρ.
Jesus the Word of God : the Saviour.

Ἰησοῦς · Μεσσίας · Θεὸς ἀληθινὸς ἐκ Θεοῦ ἀληθινοῦ.
Jesus : Messiah : Very God of Very God.

Ἰησοῦς ὁ Ἀμὴν · ὁ Λόγος κατὰ τὴν γνῶσιν.
  Jesus the Amen : the Word according to the
  Gnosis.
Ἰησοῦς ὁ Υἱὸς ἐκ Πνεύματος Ἁγίου.
  Jesus the Son from the Holy Ghost.
Μυστικὸς Λόγος · Υἱὸς Κυρίου.
  Mystic Word : Son of the Lord.
Μυστικὴ θυσία τοῦ Μεσσίου.
  Mystic Sacrifice of the Messiah.
Ἡ εἰκὼν τοῦ Πνεύματος Ἁγίου.
  The Image of the Holy Ghost.
Ὁ τεχθεὶς βασιλεὺς · ὁ Υἱὸς μονογενής.
  He that is born a King : the Only-begotten Son.
Πλήρωμα · ἡ δύναμις τοῦ Πατρός.
  Fulness : the Power of the Father.
Σωτήρ · Εἰκὼν Κυρίου.
  Saviour : Image of the Lord.
Σωτήρ · Κύριος μόνος ἐκ μόνου.
  Saviour : Only Lord of Only.
Ὁ Σωτὴρ · Κύριος ζωῆς.
  The Saviour : Lord of Life.
Φῶς κατὰ τὴν γνῶσιν.
  Light according to the Gnosis.
Φῶς · Πανμυστήριον Θεοῦ.
  Light : All-Mystery of God.
Φῶς · Ἐγὼ Εἰμὶ · Ὁ Ὤν.
  Light : I Am that I Am.
Φῶς · τὸ νόημα τοῦ Θεοῦ.
  Light : the Thought of God.
Γνῶσις ἐκ τοῦ Θεοῦ Πατρός.
  Gnosis from God the Father.
Μέγα φῶς · λόγος Κυρίου ἐνεργής.
  Great Light : Powerful Word of the Lord.
Καταβολὴ τῶν αἰώνων.
  Creation of the Aeons.

3330 Λόγος Πρῶτος καὶ Ἔσχατος.
= 37 × 90 Word First and Last.

'Ο ζῶν Λόγος ἐκ τοῦ Θεοῦ Πατρός.
The Living Word from God the Father.

Θεὸς ἀληθινὸς ἐκ τῆς οὐσίας τοῦ Θεοῦ.
Very God of the Substance of God.

Χαρὶς Κυρίου· σωτηρία.
Grace of the Lord : Salvation.

Κύριος τῶν Κυρίων.
Lord of Lords.

Ὤμεγα· φῶς σοφίας.
Omega : Light of Wisdom.

'Η ἐπένδυσις Ἰησοῦ Χριστοῦ.
The Putting-on of Jesus Christ.

Σημεῖον σωτηρίας εἰς γνῶσιν.
Token of Salvation unto Knowledge.

'Η γνῶσις· πλήρωμα Κυρίου.
The Gnosis : Fulness of the Lord.

Μυστικὴ ἐκκλησία γνώσεως.
Mystic Church of Knowledge.

Σοφία· μέγα φῶς Κυρίου.
Wisdom : Great Light of the Lord.

'Ο καλὸς λόγος τῆς γνώσεως.
The Good Word of Knowledge.

Αἷμα Χριστοῦ· μυστικὴ θυσία.
Blood of Christ : Mystic Sacrifice.

'Η εὐχαριστία τοῦ Μεσσίου.
The Eucharist of the Messiah.

Παρακλήτωρ ἀνθρώπων.
Comforter of Men.

Φῶς· Πνεῦμα τοῦ Θεοῦ.
Light : Spirit of God.

Πραγμάτων ἐλεγμὸς* οὐ βλεπομένων.
The Evidence of Things not seen (Ep. Heb. xi. 1).

Μυστήριον γεωμετρίας Ἰησοῦ.
Mystery of the Geometry of Jesus.

Φῶς· πνεῦμα καὶ δύναμις Ἠλίου.
Light : Spirit and Power of Elias.

3367   Αἷμα Χριστοῦ· ἡ εὐχαριστία.
= 37 × 91   Blood of Christ : the Eucharist.

Αἷμα Ἰησοῦ· εὐχαριστία Κυρίου.
Blood of Christ : the Lord's Eucharist.

Αἷμα Ἰησοῦ· τὸ εὐαγγέλιον Χριστοῦ.
Blood of Jesus : the Gospel of Christ.

Αἷμα Χριστοῦ· ἡ διδαχὴ Κυρίου.
Blood of Christ : the Lord's Teaching.

Σὰρξ καὶ αἷμα· ἡ πρόθεσις τοῦ σταύρου.
Flesh and Blood : the Shew-bread of the Cross.

Σὰρξ καὶ αἷμα· σῶμα τοῦ Θεοῦ· ἡ θυσία.
Flesh and Blood : Body of God : the Sacrifice.

Χριστὸς τὸ Ἄρνιον· Θεὸς μεθ' ἡμῶν.
Christ the Lamb : God with Us.

Χριστὸς τὸ Ἄρνιον· Θεότης Ἐμμανουήλ.
Christ the Lamb : Godhead : Emmanuel.

Ζωὴ· τὸ σῶμα καὶ τὸ αἷμα Ἰησοῦ.
Life : the Body and Blood of Jesus.

Ἰησοῦς· τὸ αἷμα τῆς καίνης διαθήκης Κυρίου.
Jesus : the Blood of the New Testament of the Lord.

Τὸ θυσιαστήριον· τὸ δεῖπνον Κυρίου.
The Altar : the Lord's Supper.

---

* Ἐλεγμός is the reading we suggest. See Ep. Heb. loco citato. The ordinary reading ἔλεγχος is very difficult, and gave no gematria. F. B. B. suggested ἐλεγμός (from Timothy) and the results are excellent for the whole passage.

Δεῖπνον Κυρίου · τὸ φῶς ἀληθινόν.
Lord's Supper : The True Light.

Ὁ ἄρτος · ἡ σὰρξ Κυρίου · ἡ θυσία ἐν τῇ κλάσει.
The Bread the Lord's Flesh : the Sacrifice in
the Breaking.

Ἡ στερεὰ τροφὴ τοῦ Κυρίου.
The Strong Meat of the Lord.

Πανμυστήριον γνώσεως.
All-Mystery of Knowledge.

Λόγος Φῶτος · λόγος Πατρός.
Word of Light : Word of the Father.

Ἡ γεωμετρία · ὁ λόγος κατὰ Χριστὸν.
The Geometria : the Word according to Christ.

Δημιουργὸς καὶ τεχνίτης ὁ Ἰησοῦς.
Jesus the Maker and Builder.

3 404   Κύριος Θεὸς ὁ Ὢν καὶ ὁ Ἦν καὶ ὁ Ἐρχόμενος.
= 37 × 92   Lord God Who Is and Who Was and Who
            Shall Be.

Γνῶσις Κυρίου αἰώνιος.
Eternal Knowledge of the Lord.

Ἄλφα καὶ Ὠμεγα · λόγος σωτηρίας.
First and Last : Word of Salvation.

Χριστὸς Κύριος · λόγος Πατρός.
Christ the Lord : Word of the Father.

Ἡ πᾶσα ἐξουσία Ἰησοῦ Χριστοῦ.
The All-Authority of Jesus Christ.

Εὐαγγέλιον βασιλείας Ἰησοῦ Χριστοῦ.
Gospel of the Kingdom of Jesus Christ.

Ἐνιαυτὸς Ἰησοῦ Χριστοῦ.
Era of Jesus Christ.

Φῶς Θεοῦ · ὁ λύχνος.
Light of God : the Lamp.

Καλὴ δύναμις τοῦ φῶτος.
Good Power of Light.

Ἡ ψυχὴ Κυρίου Ἰησοῦ.
The Soul of the Lord Jesus.

Τὸ Πνεῦμα τοῦ Κυρίου Ἰησοῦ.
The Spirit of the Lord Jesus.

Σκήνωσις τοῦ Πνεύματος.
Tabernacle of the Spirit.

Τὸ βάπτισμα τοῦ Ἁγίου Πνεύματος.
The Baptism of the Holy Ghost.

Ἡ σφραγίς· μυστήριον βαπτίσματος.
The Seal : Mystery of Baptism.

Κιβωτὸς· σημεῖον σωτηρίας.
An Ark : Sign of Salvation.

Σὰρξ καὶ αἷμα· Υἱὸς τοῦ ἀνθρώπου.
Flesh and Blood : Son of Man.

Ἰησοῦς ἡ πᾶσα δύναμις τοῦ Πατρός.
Jesus the All-Power of the Father.

Ἰησοῦς ὁ πνευματικὸς Νύμφιος.
Jesus the spiritual Bridegroom.

Ἰησοῦς· Ἐξουσία τοῦ Κυρίου.
Jesus : Authority of the Lord.

3441   Θεὸς τῶν ζώντων.
= 37 × 93   God of the Living.

Ἄρχων ἀνθρώπων.
Ruler of Men.

Πρωτότοκος Υἱὸς Πατρός.
First-begotten Son of the Father.

Χριστὸς ὁ Μεσσίας Θεοῦ Πατρός.
Christ the Messiah of God the Father.

Φῶς ἐκ τοῦ Πνεύματος.
Light from the Spirit.

Ἐπουράνιος εἰκὼν τοῦ κόσμου.
Celestial Image of the Cosmos.

Ἀρχιερεὺς κατὰ τὴν τάξιν Μελχισεδέκ.
Priest after the Order of Melchisedec.

Ἐσώτερον ὄνομα Χριστοῦ.
Esoteric Name of Christ.

Ἰησοῦς τὸ ἔσω μυστήριον.
Jesus the Inward Mystery.

Μυστήριον Θεοῦ · σφαῖρα τῆς βασιλείας.
Ἡ σφαῖρα τῶν οὐρανῶν.
The Sphere of the Heavens.

Σημεῖον τῶν μυστηρίων.
Sign of the Mysteries.

Σημεῖον γνώσεως Κυρίου.
Sign of the Knowledge of the Lord.

Ὁ Κηφᾶς · μυστήριον γεωμετρίας.
Cephas : Mystery of Geometry.

Πλήρωμα θεότητος · ὁ λύχνος.
Fulness of the Godhead : the Lamp.

Περιστερὰ τοῦ φωτός.
Dove of Light.

Τὸ φῶς τοῦ Α · Ω.
The Light of the First and Last.

Γνῶσις · μυστήριον Κυρίου.
Gnosis : Mystery of the Lord.

3478 Τὸ σωτήριον τοῦ κόσμου.
= 37 × 94 The Salvation of the World.

Λόγος φῶτος Θεοῦ Πατρός.
Word of Light of God the Father.

Or, Τὸ φῶς · Λόγος Θεοῦ Πατρός.
Light : the Word of Light of God the Father.

Κύριος σωτηρίας · Πλήρωμα.
Lord of Salvation : Fulness.

Κύριος σωτηρίας · Πατρότης.
Κύριος σωτηρίας · μέγας Παράκλητος.
Φῶς · μυστήριον κόσμου.
Light : Mystery of the World.

Τὸ μυστικὸν φῶς ἡλίου.
The Mystic Light of the Sun.

Ἐξανάστασις τοῦ Χριστοῦ.
Resurrection of Christ.

Μυστήριον τῶν ζ' ἐκκλησίων.
Mystery of the Seven Churches.

Πᾶσα ἐξουσία τοῦ Χριστοῦ.
All-Authority of Christ.

Ἡ σφραγὶς τῆς γεωμετρίας Θεοῦ.
The Seal of the Geometry of God.

Μυστήριον γεωμετρίας ἐπουράνιον.
Heavenly Mystery of Geometry.

Τέλειος Κύριος γνώσεως.
Perfect Lord of Knowledge.

Ὁ Πρωινὸς Ἀστὴρ τῆς σοφίας.
The Morning Star of Wisdom.

Ὁ Λόγος τῆς σοφίας ἐκ τοῦ Πατρός.
The Word of Wisdom from the Father.

Τὰ πάντα καὶ ἐν πᾶσι ·Ἰησοῦς Χριστός.
All and In All : Jesus Christ.

Ἰησοῦς · μυστικὸν φῶς.
Jesus : Mystic Light.

Ἰησοῦς · μυστικὸς λύχνος.
Jesus : Mystic Lamp.

Ἰησοῦς · Ἄλφα καὶ Ὤμεγα μυστήριον.
Jesus the First and Last Mystery.

Ἰησοῦς ·Ἱερεὺς φωτός.
Jesus : Priest of Light.

Ἰησοῦς · Α · Ω · ἡ σοφία Κυρίου.
Jesus : First : Last : Wisdom of the Lord.

Ἰησοῦς πανμυστήριον χάριτος.
Jesus : All-Mystery of Grace.

Ἰησοῦς ὁ προφητὴς τοῦ Θεοῦ.
Jesus the Prophet of God.

Ἰησοῦς ὁ Λόγος · ἡ εἰκὼν τοῦ Θεοῦ.
Jesus the Word : the Image of God.

3515   Κύριος Θεὸς τῶν πάντων.
= 37 × 95   Lord God of All.

Κύριος Χριστὸς Θεοῦ Πατρὸς.
Lord Anointed of God the Father.

Θεὸς πάντων · ὁ ὕψιστος.
Lord of All : the Highest.

Ἐκπόρευσις Πνεύματος ἐκ τοῦ Θεοῦ.
Procession of the Spirit from God.

Τὸ μυστήριον τῆς βασιλείας Κυρίου.
The Mystery of the Kingdom of the Lord.

Ἰησοῦς Χριστὸς · καταβολὴ Παρθένου.
Jesus Christ : Conception of a Virgin.

Χριστὸς ὁ Υἱὸς τῆς ἀγάπης Θεοῦ.
Christ, the Son of God's Love.

Οὐσία ἄπειρος · ὁ Θεὸς τῶν Θεῶν.
Infinite Essence : the God of Gods.

Χριστὸς · Λόγος Θεοῦ · μυστήριον.
Christ : Word of God : Mystery.

Χριστὸς · Σοφία τοῦ Θεοῦ.
Christ : Wisdom of God.

Χριστὸς · εὐαγγέλιον τοῦ Ἰησοῦ.
Christ : Gospel of Jesus.

Χριστὸς · γνῶσις τῆς ἀληθείας.
Christ : Knowledge of Truth.

Χριστὸς · τὸ ῥῆμα ἐνσώματον.
Christ the Word Incarnate.

Χριστὸς · Μεσίτης · Μονογενὴς ἐκ Πατρός.
Christ : Mediator : Only-begotten of the Father.

Χριστὸς ὁ Ναζωραῖος · ὁ Μεσσίας.
Christ the Nazarene : the Messiah.

Χριστὸς ὁ Κτιστὴς ὁ ζῶν.
Christ the Living Creator.

Χριστὸς · ἱλασμὸς Κυρίου Θεοῦ.
Christ : Propitiation of the Lord God.

Τὸ πρόσωπον τοῦ Μεσσίου.
Χριστὸς ὁ Ὑιὸς · ἀληθὴς Λόγος · Μεσσίας.
  Christ the Son : True Word : Messiah.

Ἑνότης Θεοτήτος Κυρίου · ὁ Ὤν.
  Unity of the Godhead of the Lord : He Who Is.

Ἰησοῦς Σωτήρ · ὁ Λόγος ἐκ Πατρός.
  Jesus : Saviour : the Word from the Father.

Φῶς Θεοῦ · ὁ γεωμέτρης.
  Light of God : Geometer.

Λόγος φωτός · ἡ γεωμετρία.
  Word of Light : Geometry.

Ἡ σφραγὶς τοῦ γεωμέτρου.
  The Seal of the Geometer.

Πλήρωμα τῆς γεωμετρίας Θεοῦ.
  Fulness of the Geometry of God.

Ὁ τεχνίτης τῆς γεωμετρίας.
  The Maker of Geometry.

Ἰησοῦς ὁ Ὑιὸς τῆς ἀγάπης Θεοῦ.
  Jesus the Son of the Love of God.

3552 Λόγος φωτός · πανμυστήριον.
= 37 × 96 Word of Light : All-Mystery.

Φῶς · παντελεία τοῦ κόσμου.
  Light : Consummation of the Universe.

Τὸ φῶς · τὸ ἅγιον μυστήριον.
  Light : the Holy Mystery.

Τὸ φῶς · τὸ μάννα τὸ κεκρυμμένον.
  Light : the Hidden Manna.

Ὁ Ναζωραῖος · λόγος φωτός.
  The Nazarene : Word of Light.

Κύριος Θεός · τὸ φῶς τὸ ἀληθινόν.
  Lord God : the True Light.

Ὁ Ζῶν Κύριος · ἡ ἀνάστασις καὶ ἡ ζωή.
  The Living Lord : the Resurrection and the
    Life.

'Ο Λόγος· ἀρχηγὸς τῆς σωτηρίας.
The Word : Captain of Salvation.

Χριστὸς τὸ ἄλφα· τὸ Ω.
Christ : the First : the Last.

'Η καινὴ φιλοσοφία· γεωμετρία κόσμου.
The New Philosophy : Geometry of the Universe.

Χριστὸς· ἡ γεωμετρία κόσμου.
Christ : Geometry of the Universe.

'Ο μέγας Γεωμέτρης τῆς ἀληθείας Κυρίου.
The Great Geometer of the Lord's Truth.

Μέγας Γεωμέτρης· φωνὴ Θεοῦ.
Great Geometer : Voice of God.

Μέγας Γεωμέτρης· φόβος Κυρίου.
Great Geometer : Fear of the Lord.

Μέγας Γεωμέτρης· αἰὼν σοφίας.
Great Geometer : Aeon of Wisdom.

Μέγας Γεωμέτρης· ἐπίγνωσις Θεοῦ.
Great Geometer : Knowledge of God.

'Ο μέγας Γεωμέτρης· ἡ κλῖμαξ τοῦ Ἰακώβ.
The Great Geometer : Jacob's Ladder.

'Ο μέγας Γεωμέτρης· ὁ λόγος ἐξ Αἰγύπτου.
The Great Geometer : the word out of Egypt.

'Ο μέγας Γεωμέτρης· ὁ ἀρχάγγελος Μιχαήλ.
The Great Geometer : the Archangel Michael.

'Ο μέγας Γεωμέτρης· δρόμος τοῦ ἡλίου.
The Great Geometer : Course of the Sun.

3589
= 37 × 97 'Η Σωτηρία λαῶν πάντων.
The Salvation of All Peoples.

Καταπέτασμα ναοῦ σχιστὸν εἰς δύο.
The Veil of the Temple rent in Twain.

'Η παρουσία· τὸ ἄστρον ἐκ τοῦ Ἰακώβ.
The Coming : the Star out of Jacob.

Γνῶσις· παρουσία γεωμετρίας.
Gnosis : Advent of Geometry.

Παρουσία Κυρίου· ἡ γνῶσις κατά Θεόν.
  Coming of the Lord : the Gnosis of God.

Παρουσία Κυρίου· ἡ τετάρτη δύναμις.
  Coming of the Lord : the Fourth Power (geo-
    metrical).

Ἡ παρουσία Κυρίου· ὁ τετάρτος λόγος.
  The Coming of the Lord : the Fourth Power
    or factor (mathematical).

Παρουσία Θεοῦ· λόγος φωτός.
  Coming of God : Word of Light.

Ἡ παρουσία τοῦ Θεοῦ· ἡ οἰκουμένη ἡ μέλλουσα.
  The Coming of God : the World to Come.

Ὁ Θεὸς ἐρχόμενος· ὁ Λόγος κατὰ Χριστὸν.
  The God that shall come : the Word according
    to Christ.

Λόγος μυστηρίου Ἰησοῦ Κυρίου.
  Word of the Mystery of the Lord Jesus.

Λόγος κατὰ μυστήριον· Τεκτόναρχος.
  Word according to the Mystery : Master-
    Builder.

Μελχισεδὲκ· Κύριος φωτός.
  Melchisedec : Lord of Light.

Ἄλφα· Ὠμεγα· Σωτὴρ κόσμου.
  First : Last : Saviour of the World.

Κύριος Σαβαώθ· Ἀποκάλυψις Ἀληθείας.
  Lord of Hosts : Revelation of Truth.

Ἡ ἐπιφανεία τοῦ Θεοῦ ἐν μορφῇ κύβου.
  (See Clem. Hom. xvii, attributed to St. Peter.)

Κηφᾶς ὁ πέτρος· ὁ μέγας τεκτόναρχος.
Πέτρος ὁ κύβος· ἡ ἐκκλησία τοῦ Κυρίου.
Πεντέρημα· φῶς κατὰ μυστήριον.

Γνῶσις· ὁ Σωτὴρ· Βασιλεύς.
  Knowledge : the Saviour King.

Ὁ Σωτὴρ· Ποιμὴν ἄνδρων· Βασιλεύς.
  The Saviour : Shepherd of Men : King.

3626 Ὁ Πρωτότοκος ἐκ τοῦ Πατρός.
= 37 × 98   The First-Begotten of the Father.

Ὁ Ἰησοῦς* ἐκ τῆς οὐσίας τοῦ Θεοῦ.
    Jesus of the Substance of God.

Οὐσία τοῦ Θεοῦ · ὁ λόγος ἐκ τῆς Παρθένου.
    Substance of God : the Word from the Virgin

Τὸ Ἅγιον Πνεῦμα ἐκ τοῦ Κύριου Πατρὸς.
    The Holy Ghost from the Lord the Father.

Τὸ Πνεῦμα Χριστοῦ Κυρίου.
    The Spirit of the Lord Christ.

Θεὸς Σωτὴρ · Ὑιὸς τοῦ Θεοῦ.
    God the Saviour : Son of God.

Ἰησοῦς Ὑιὸς γνώσεως.
    Jesus : Son of Gnosis.

Ὁ Σωτὴρ · Ποιμὴν ἀνθρώπων.
    The Saviour : Shepherd of Men.

Μυστήριον τοῦ Σωτῆρος.
    Mystery of the Saviour.

Μεσσίας τοῦ Θεοῦ · Τεκτόναρχος.
    Messiah of God : Master-Builder.

Λόγος φωτός · σημεῖον Κυρίου.
    Word of Light : Sign of the Lord

3663 Τὸ φῶς · πανμυστήριον Θεοῦ.
= 37 × 99   Light : All-Mystery of God.

Λόγος φωτός · ὁ λύχνος.
    Word of Light : the Lamp.

Μέγας λύχνος τῶν ἐθνῶν.
    Great Light of the Peoples.

Τὸ φῶς κατὰ τὴν γνῶσιν.
    The Light according to the Gnosis.

Φῶς · ὁ Μιχαὴλ καὶ οἱ ἄγγελοι αὐτοῦ.
    Light : Michael and his Angels.

---

* Alternatively παρθένος λόγος = 888.

Ἀγγελιαρχὸς τοῦ Φωτός.
Archangel of Light.

Χριστὸς Μεσίτης · ὁ λύχνος.
Christ the Mediator : the Lamp.

Χριστὸς ἡ δύναμις τῆς Θεότητος.
Christ the Power of the Godhead.

Χριστὸς · Πλήρωμα · Λόγος Πατρός.
Christ : Pleroma : Word of the Father.

Ἰησοῦς ἡ ἐνανθρώπησις τοῦ Θεοῦ.
Jesus the Incarnation of God.

Ἰησοῦς · Ἐπίσκοπος τῶν ἀνθρώπων.
Jesus : Bishop of Men.

Ὁ Ἀρχηγὸς τῆς σωτηρίας Θεοῦ.
The Captain of the Salvation of God.

Ἀληθινός Ἐπίσκοπος ψυχῶν.
True Bishop of Souls.

Α καὶ Ω · Σημεῖον τοῦ Σωτῆρος.
First and Last : Sign of the Saviour.

Γνῶσις τοῦ Ἁγίου Πνεύματος.
Knowledge of the Holy Ghost.

Ὁ ἐνδιάθετος Λόγος τῆς γνώσεως.
The Implanted Word of Knowledge.

Ἐκπόρευσις Πνεύματος · ἡ σωτηρία.
Procession of the Spirit : Salvation.

Τελείωσις σωτηρίας Θεοῦ.
Perfecting of the Salvation of God.

Ἰησοῦς Χριστὸς · διαθήκη Θεοῦ Πατρός.
Jesus Christ : Covenant of God the Father.

3700 Ὁ Χριστὸς τὸ Πάσχα ἡμῶν.
= 37 × 100 Christ Our Passover.

Σωτήριον λαῶν Πάντων.
Salvation of All Peoples.

Ἰχθὺς · σύμβολον σωτηρίας.
A Fish : Emblem of Salvation.

Τὸ Πάσχα τοῦ Σωτῆρος.
The Saviour's Passover.

Λόγος γνώσεως· δεῖπνον Κυρίου.
Word of Knowledge : the Lord's Supper.

Σοφία Ὑιοῦ· δεῖπνον τοῦ Κυρίου.
Wisdom of the Son : the Lord's Supper.

Τὸ Σωτήριον· δεῖπνον τῆς ζωῆς.
The Salvation : Supper of Life.

Τὸ νοερὸν πνεῦμα· τὸ δεῖπνον τοῦ Κυρίου.
The Spirit of Intelligence : the Lord's Supper.

Τὸ φῶς· Πνεῦμα τοῦ Θεοῦ.
Light : the Spirit of God.

Ἀστὴρ Χριστοῦ φαίνων.
Star of Christ appearing.

Δήλωσις τοῦ Σωτῆρος.
Manifestation of the Saviour.

Φῶς σοφίας· ὁ Λόγος ἐκ Πατρός.
Light of Wisdom : Word of the Father.

Φῶς Πρῶτον Κόσμου.
First Light of the World.

Πρῶτον ἔνταλμα· Λόγος κατὰ μυστήριον.
First Precept : Word according to the Mystery.

Ἡ γνῶσις Κυρίου· τὸ πλήρωμα.
The Knowledge of the Lord : the Fulness.

Μέγα φῶς τοῦ Ἰωάννου.
Great Light of John.

Τὸ μέγα φῶς· σοφία Κυρίου.
The Great Light : Wisdom of the Lord.

Τὸ μέγα φῶς· Λόγος Σωτήρ.
The Great Light : the Saving Word.

3737 Ὁ Ἰχθὺς τοῦ Σωτῆρος.
= 37 × 101 The Fish (symbol) of the Saviour.

Τὸ Ὄνομα Ἰησοῦ τοῦ Σωτῆρος.
The Name of Jesus the Saviour.

Ἰησοῦς Χριστὸς εἰκὼν Θεοῦ.
Jesus Christ : Image of God.

Τὸ φῶς · σημεῖον Κυρίου Θεοῦ.
Light the Sign of the Lord God.

Ἡ Σοφία · μυστήριον τοῦ Κυρίου.
Wisdom : Mystery of the Lord.

Χριστὸς τὸ σωτήριον Ἰσραήλ.
Christ the Salvation of Israel.

Φωσφόρος ἀστὴρ Ἰησοῦ.
Light-bringing Star of Jesus.

Πλρωμα σωτηρίας · Μέγας Παράκλητος.
Fulness of Salvation : Great Paraclete.

Νόμος σωτηρίας Κυρίου Ἰησοῦ.
Law of Salvation of the Lord Jesus.

Ἡ Σὰρξ Κυρίου Ἰησοῦ Χριστοῦ.
The Flesh of the Lord Jesus Christ.

Ἄλφα μυστήριον · Ὠμεγα μυστήριον.
First Mystery : Last Mystery.

Ἄλφα · Ω · ὁ Σωτὴρ ὁ Ζῶν.
First : Last : the Living Saviour.

Ἄλφα · Ω · ἡ μυστικὴ σωτηρία.
First : Last : the Mystic Salvation.

Ἄλφα · Ω · τὸ εὐαγγέλιον τοῦ Ἰησοῦ.
First : Last : the Gospel of Jesus.

3774 Ὁ Μεσσίας · ὁ Σωτὴρ τοῦ κόσμου.
= 37 × 102 The Messiah : the Saviour of the World.

Ἰησοῦς Χριστὸς ἐν σώματι.
Jesus Christ in the Flesh.

Χριστὸς · Πλήρωμα Θεοῦ Πατρός.
Christ : Fulness of God the Father.

Τὸ φῶς Θεοῦ · ὁ λύχνος.
Tho Light of God : the Lamp.

Τὸ ἅγιον φῶς τοῦ Κυρίου.
The Holy Light of the Lord.

Λόγος φωτός · ὁ γεωμέτρης.
    Word of Light : the Geometer.

Ὁ Ναζωραῖος · Ὑιὸς τοῦ τέκτονος.
    The Nazarene : Son of the Carpenter.

Ἄλφα καὶ Ὠμεγα · φῶς τῆς ἡμέρας.
    First and Last : Light of the Day.

Ὁ ἄγρος · ὁ σῖτος · τὸ ἄχυρον · ἡ ἅλων.
    The Field : the Corn : the Chaff : the Threshing-
    floor.

Ὁ ἄρτος · ἡ κοινωνία τῶν ἁγίων.
    The Bread : the Communion of the Saints.

Ἀληθινὸν μυστήριον Ἰησοῦ Χριστοῦ.
    True Mystery of Jesns Christ.

Ἰησοῦς Χριστὸς ὁ Ὑιὸς · Μεσσίας.
    Jesus Christ, the Son : Messiah.

3811   Φῶς · πρῶτον ἔνταλμα Θεοῦ.
= 37 × 103   Light : First Precept of God.

Γνῶσις · τὸ μυστήριον Κυρίου.
    Gnosis is the Mystery of the Lord.

Τὸ σημεῖον τῶν μυστήριων.
    The Sign of the Mysteries.

Σταύρος · σύμβολον Σωτῆρος.
    A Cross : Symbol of the Saviour.

Ὁ Μεσίτης · Σωτὴρ τοῦ κόσμου.
    The Mediator : Saviour of the World.

Φῶς · οὐσία πνεύματος Θεοῦ.
    Light : Substance of the Spirit.

Ὁ Χριστὸς · γεωμέτρης κόσμου.
    Christ : Geometer of the World of God.

Ἡ γεωμετρία · αἰὼν Σωτῆρος.
    Geometry : Aeon of the Saviour.

Μυστικὸν σῶμα Χριστοῦ.
    Mystical Body of Christ.

Ζῶν Θεός · Κύριος φωτός.
 Living God! Lord of Light.

Ἰησοῦς Χριστὸς ὁ Λόγος Κυρίου.
 Jesus Christ the Word of the Lord.

Ἰησοῦς Χριστὸς · Υἱὸς · Μεσίτης.
 Jesus Christ : Son : Mediator.

Βοὴ ἐκ ἐρήμῳ · κήρυγμα τοῦ Ἰωάννου.
 A Cry in the Wilderness : Preaching of John
  Baptist.

Κύριος φωτός αἰώνιος.
 Eternal Lord of Light.

Νόμος τῆς σωτηρίας τοῦ Θεοῦ.
 Law of the Salvation of God.

3848 Ὁ Κύριος Σωτὴρ τοῦ κόσμου.
= 37 × 104 The Lord : Saviour of the World.

Ἰησοῦς Υἱὸς τοῦ ἀνθρώπου.
 Jesus : Son of Man.

Πλήρωμα φωτός · ὄνομα Ἰησοῦ.
 Fulness of Light : Name of Jesus.

Πλήρωμα φωτός · ἡ χαρὶς.
 Fulness of Light : Grace.

Σφραγὶς πνεύματος Κυρίου Ἰησοῦ.
 Seal of the Spirit of the Lord Jesus.

Τὸ φῶς · μυστήριον κόσμου.
 Light : Mystery of the Cosmos.

Ὁ ἀστὴρ τῆς ἀγάπης Ἰησοῦ Χριστοῦ.

Α · Ω · ὁ ἀστὴρ Ἰησοῦ Χριστοῦ.

Ὁ κύβος Κυρίου · ἡ ἀπόρροια τοῦ ἄστερος.

Ἰησοῦς ἡ ανάστασις · τὸ ἄστρον ἐξ Ἰακώβ.
 Jesus the Resurrection : Star out of Jacob.

3885 Ἡ σωτηρία τοῦ Κυρίου Ἰησοῦ.
= 37 × 105 The Salvation of the Lord Jesus.

Ὁ Ἐνσώματος Λόγος ἐκ Κυρίου Πατρός.
  The Incarnate Word from God the Father.

Δύναμις καὶ σοφία Ἰησοῦ Χριστοῦ.
  Power and Wisdom of Jesus Christ.

Χριστὸς ὁ Σωτήρ · ὁ Λόγος Θεοῦ.
  Christ the Saviour : the Word of God.

Χριστὸς μυστικὴ σωτηρία.
  Christ the Mystic Salvation.

Ἰησοῦς Χριστὸς Κύριος ἐκ Μαρίας γεννηθείς.
  Jesus Christ : Lord born of Mary.

Τὸ πλήρωμα τῆς γεωμετρίας Θεοῦ.
  The Fulness of the Geometry of God.

Γεωμετρία τῶν οὐρανῶν.
  Geometry of the Heavens.

Ἡ τελείωσις τῶν ἡγιασμένων.
  The Perfecting of the Sanctified.

Κύριος Ἰησοῦς · ὁ Σωτὴρ τῆς γῆς.

3922 Ἡ σωτηρία τῶν Ἰουδαίων.
= 37 × 106 The Salvation of the Jews.

Ἰησοῦς Χριστὸς · ἀνάστασις σαρκός.
  Jesus Christ the Resurrection of the Flesh.

Τὸ σωτήριον τῶν ἁγιων.
  The Salvation of the Saints.

Κύριος Ἰησοῦς · ἡ δύναμις τοῦ Πατρός.
  Lord Jesus : the Power of the Father.

Φῶς · θησαυρὸς Θεοῦ κεκρυμμένος.
  Light : Hidden Treasury of God.

3959   Λόγος φῶτος τεκτόναρχος.
= 37 × 107   Word of Light : Master-builder.

'Ο Χριστὸς · δημιουργὸς καὶ τεχνίτης.
   Christ : Maker and Builder.

Φῶς κόσμου · λύχνος ἐκ Θεοῦ.
   Light of the World : Lamp from God.

Χαρὶς · ὁ σωτὴρ τοῦ κόσμου.
   Grace : the Saviour of the World.

'Η κατόρθωσις τοῦ σταύρου.
   The Setting-up of the Cross.

'Ο Λόγος τοῦ Κυρίου · κόκκος σινάπεως.
   The Word of the Lord : a Grain of Mustard.

3996   Τὸ μυστήριον τοῦ σωτῆρος.
= 37 × 108   The Mystery of the Saviour.

Φῶς ἡλίου · μυστήριον κόσμου.
   Light of the Sun : Mystery of the World.

Λύχνος ἐκ τῶν οὐρανῶν.
   Lamp from the Heavens.

'Ο λύχνος ἐν τῷ οὐρανῷ.
   Lamp in the Heavens.

Α · Ω · 'Αμὴν · 'Ιησοῦς σωτὴρ κόσμου.
Θησαυρὸς γνώσεως κεκρύμμενος.
   Hidden Treasury of Knowledge.

Φῶς Θεοῦ · ἅρμα φωτός.
   Light of God : Chariot of Light.

Φῶς καθάρσιον · τεῖχος πυρός.
   Cleansing Light : Wall of Fire.

3996.

With this number we terminate the present
series. It might be continued indefinitely
above the 4000 limit, and there are many
very significant instances of Biblical and traditional gematria upon the higher numbers, but these we

37 × 108
36 × 111
6 × 666
1272 × π

are constrained for the present to withhold. In the selection we have here given it will be possible for readers to discern evidence of various orders of symbolism, astronomical, architectural, and otherwise, in which is veiled the mystery of Jesus Christ as the Incarnate Word and the Maker of the Aeons of Time and Space. The Messiahship, the Divine-Human nature, alone perfectly expressed in Him, is the heritage of the whole race of Man, and the Geometry of the Cubic Stone, never seen in its fulness by the physical eye save as the metacubic Hexagon, is the central type of His All-presence in cosmic order and creative function. But the higher Mind can apprehend the greater truth of the symbol, and the Ideal being the only Reality, it is in the forming of the human soul in the image of His perfect Symmetry that the power is given to comprehend the inwardness of all those manifested symmetries of Nature which appeal to the student of the Divine principles as tokens of the omnipresence of God in His universe.

The number 3996 is geometrical, but chiefly in astronomical allusion and is pre-eminently the symbol of that grand Circle of cosmic days which is Six times the Solar cycle of 666. We shall hope to explain in a later publication how this mystery is revealed from the Biblical text, as well as from the philosophic tradition and gnostic numerologies.

3996 is the Circle whose diameter is 1272, just as both in Hebrew and Greek Cabala the Circle 666 (really 666·66, etc.) has the diameter 212—the Hebrew HOR, the Light, and the Greek ὅραμα (Horama), the Vision of God in the Burning Bush. But we shall also shew thnt even that uniquely perfect calculus of the Circle, the Ratio of Metius so-called, was familiar to the inspired writers and that gematria based on that ratio (113:355) takes the place, in the part of the Scriptures devoted to the astronomical calculus, of that more universally known reckoning, associated with the Mystery of 666. We conclude with a selection of miscellaneous gematria on 3996. It is only a small part of what we might give.

3996 Ἐνιαυτὸς ἡλίου · ἡ ἐξουσία Κυρίου Ἰησοῦ.
= 37 × 106 Era of the Sun : the Authority of the Lord Jesus.

Ἐνιαυτὸς ἡλιου · Κήρυγμα φωτός.
Era of Elias (John) : Preaching of Light.

Ἥλιος δικαιοσύνης · ὁ Λόγος τοῦ Θεοῦ Κύριου.
Sun of Righteousness : the Word of the Lord God.

Ἡ πρώτη διαθήκη τοῦ φωτός.
The First Covenant of Light.

Α · Ω · ὁ ἐνιαυτὸς ὁ μέγας τοῦ Κυρίου.
First : Last : the Great Era of the Lord.

Μέγας αἰών · ἀστρονομικὸς ἐνιαυτὸς τῆς γῆς.
Great Aeon : Astronomical Era of the Earth.

Ἰησοῦς Χριστὸς · Ἀναγέννησις ἐκ νέκρων.
Jesus Christ : Resurrection from the dead.

Ἡ μεγάλη ἡμέρα · ἐνιαυτὸς τῆς γῆς · ἀστρονομικὸς αἰών.
The Great Day : Era of the Earth : astronomic Aeon.

Ἡ ἐκκλησία ἡ πᾶσα · ἐνιαυτὸς Ἰησοῦ Χριστοῦ.
The Whole Church : Era of Jesus Christ.

Γεωμετρία Κυρίου · ἡ ἡμέρα τῆς Παρουσίας.
Geometry of the Lord : the Day of the Advent.

Other books published by Research into Lost
Knowledge Organisation Trust